Don't Lose Your Balance

DON'T LOSE YOUR BALANCE
Live Life or Build a Business? Do Both.
Copyright © 2024 Ron Bockstahler

ISBN: 978-1-964046-46-4

**Expert
Press**

www.ExpertPress.net

Expert Press
11610 Pleasant Ridge Rd.
Suite 103, #189
Little Rock AR 72223
www.ExpertPress.net

Editing by Tamma Ford
Copyediting by Hannah Skaggs
Proofreading by Heather Dubnick
Text design and composition by Emily Fritz
Cover design by Casey Fritz

Don't Lose Your Balance

Live Life or Build a Business?
Do Both.

Ron Bockstahler

Contents

Part II: Mid-Journey Checklist:Business Basics for a Balanced Life

Introduction

I guess in any book in which the author claims he knows something readers don't, a backstory is needed.

I'm a sales guy to my bones. I'm a goals guy down to the ground. I like to think I can see my end goal and that I've been marching toward it through the years. Seizing the opportunity to start a business as a way to live the life I wanted was a decision I made with my wonderful business partner Frank Chalupa, who has since retired from the business we started together twenty years ago. How it's still thriving and giving me a balance in life through twenty years of change in the world is what I'll be describing to you.

Serendipity has been a major force in my life, propelling me into a lifestyle that I didn't have the creativity to dream of when I was young. My idea, and what I

Serendipity has been a major force in my life.

thought I did best, was to do business the stereotypical American way: work like a government mule, just as hard as I could, waiting for the payoff or some kind of advancement.

After four years in the marines and two and a half years of college, I began a job I hadn't ever expected to do, selling copiers. I found out straight out of the gate that I wasn't particularly good at this! Still, I spent a year struggling at it.

If that sounds like an unconvincing tale, I'll drop a worse one on you: Five months went by before I sold my first copier. Yes, I was persistent and willing to learn (make that *eager* to learn), but I wasn't a naturally gifted salesman on day one.

Still, I told myself that sales would always be one of the two basic building blocks of any business, so I was in the right place. All it took was a bit of a boost and a bit of bad luck—even bad luck can be a fortuitous thing if you look at it that way—to get me on my way.

Back to serendipity. My good luck came from my manager and mentor, Doug May, who took me for a spin in his BMW one day. He pulled up to a men's clothing store, where he picked up the tab for suits, shirts, socks, and shoes for me. He said that to be a successful salesman, I had to look the part. With these new outfits, he said, I would soon make enough to pay him back for his grand gesture.

More serendipity. Not long after that, another salesman I looked up to, Roger Koeppen, handed me an order sheet that included $13,000 in commissions just to help me qualify for the President's Club—no questions asked.

I was stunned. I still know these men and frequently challenge them on their capricious generosity. I guess they thought I was a good risk. I hope they were right.

This is still, however, the story of a workaholic (salesmen are often workaholics). I worked my butt off and was promoted to manager two years after becoming a top-ranked salesman in the company. As my management skills grew, I ended up handling the mergers of several companies that became IKON (not the boy-band from South Korea). With this move, I ended up spending a year in Atlanta, Georgia, roughly 720 miles from my home in Chicago (which was a mile from Wrigley Field, as it happened). I had finally joined the C-suite of a serious company, fulfilling one of my dreams.

But one thing was clear right away: The price was too steep. Oh, I was there, in Atlanta, fulfilling one of my life's ambitions. I had gotten there with blinders on, a tireless workaholic the entire way. Only it turned out it wasn't what I had been looking for.

Is It Worth It?

I was far from my family, spending too many nights imbibing expensive beverages (drinking too much, to put it bluntly). I needed to tap my heels three times and say, "There's no place like home." And that's what I did. I took a regional position with Archer Management Services, overseeing their operations from Utah to Pittsburgh and from Minnesota to Texas. I was on the road five days a week, working a blistering schedule . . . again. Funny how that happens, huh?

But along came more serendipity: Earlier in my career I met my future partner Frank Chalupa. He was sixteen years my senior, a close friend, and a quintessential salesman—a man whose career preceded cell phones and whose arsenal, when he was coming up, had consisted of a Rolodex of contacts and a handshake.

It took a few nights at the bar to convince Frank we should throw in together. It was an adventure from the beginning. Our plan, if you could call it that, was to use our salesmanship to sell copy/print work, while we built up our outsourced management clientele. The first problem was that I knew nothing about printing, which made for some very interesting sales calls. The next issue was the non-competes we had in place preventing us from entering the outsourcing industry immediately. After a year of slowly building our client base, we saw an opportunity to take over a vacated shared office space. Looking back on those days, maybe we weren't smart enough to worry or think we could fail because within a few years, we had five shared office locations generating close to $10 million in annual revenue.

After six years of steady growth, I decided to move my family 300 miles away, to Danville, Indiana.

Now suddenly I had all the pieces in place, even if one or two of them had been completely accidental. I would run my own company remotely and figure out how to make it all work. I had to learn how to trust my employees, create efficiencies, measure business results, and manage the whole thing from a distance.

How was I going to do that? I was a big fan of self-help business books when I was starting out, and here was a chance to put all that knowledge to work. It all came down to goals.

Who Is Serving and Who Is Served?

I've always been a goals guy. Now what I wanted and needed was to prioritize my family, because I had been raised by a fairly terrific father who had taught me sticking together was Job One in the Bockstahler household. I had to start doing Job One better. Thus, goals.

Like people tend to do, I started with what I knew. And the first thing I knew was to get out paper and pencil and organize my thoughts. I wrote down my end goal, then my in-between goals. And I started in on achieving them.

When you're trying to figure out what you want in life, you should focus on your endgame. If you're thinking about starting a business, don't do it just because you hate your salaried job. Start a business for the right reason. I want to give you some insight in these pages about how to do that. I've made every mistake known to man. I'm wrong 50 percent of the time, and if I knew which 50 percent I'd be brilliant. But I've learned some valuable things that can help you build the business you want and enjoy your life.

To do this, I like to compare a business and whatever technology you use: Tech is there to serve us and our goals for efficiency, not the other way around. Likewise, your business should serve you and your life goals, not the other way around.

No one knows how to achieve that balance naturally. However, I think I can give you some good insights that will help you go out there and open that new business.

My clients are primarily lawyers, and a good portion of them are solo practitioners or small boutique firms. That's who I cater to and who I want to communicate this to: *It's not about working in your office till you die.* I believe six of my clients have done just that in the twenty years I've owned my business. They were, quite literally, in the office working another insanely long day when they died. They had all said things like, "Look, I'm going to work till I'm dead" or "I'm leaving feet first" or "Retirement?! Surely you're joking!"

It's a case of being careful what you wish for.

I think that's just crazy. An owner of any type of business might relate to these statements, and that's unfortunate. It's why I want this book to be read and understood. I'm here to tell you there's a better way.

Now, I'm pretty sure that until the very end, those business owners who died at their desks thought what they had was a great life. But at the end of the day, they missed out on so many opportunities and experiences in their personal lives. Many of them missed out on having good family relationships. Good relationships take time and attention, and they didn't even try. They went through divorces. Their kids pulled away from them. Their social circles shriveled up, and the only people they knew were the ones they worked with. They were great at their jobs, but that might be the only thing they believed they were great at, and they missed out on so much life.

Many of my clients are thinking, "Yeah, I'll put in my hours and my years and have a great retirement. I've got my bucket list all lined up." In my mind, they're missing the point.

The journey is the destination. Think about Americans— even on vacation, we forget about the journey. We hop on a plane, and it's all about the destination. What's between here and there, though? We don't know. We don't stop to smell the proverbial roses.

Because I have an RV and we've taken our kids to all fifty states as well as nine territories and provinces in Canada over an eight-year time frame, I know something about the journey. I never drove more than five hours in a day.

There was a guy who said to me after his family's first (and last, I guess) RV road trip, "Man, we rented this RV. It was horrible. We drove thirteen or sixteen hours to get here." At the time, I shook my head at that, and I'm still amazed when I think about it.

I asked him, "Why would you do that? You missed every great sight, activity, and landscape between here and South Dakota?! What was your hurry? Weren't you on vacation?"

Here's what I'm going to show you in my book: how to make a living . . . and have a life. It means you have to start with the end in mind. Let me show you how.

Part I:
Pre-journey Checklist:

Goal-Setting for a Balanced Life

Chapter 1

Start with the End in Mind

To tell you why I'm writing this book, I have to go back to why I started a business. I did it so I'd have more time.

I get it—that's not what you usually hear from a business owner. Usually it's about making more money than you could at a salaried job. Usually the business founder is all about putting in the time to make the money.

I agree that you need to go out—to a job or a business— and do what you like. It's a way to be happy. Me? I'm not doing it everyone else's way.

Doing what makes you happy is also often why a new business owner states they opened that business: They like the product or the service. That's just not good enough, either. It's not enough. It's just not enough if your real reason (after doing some digging in your mind) is something like "Getting my life back from the rat race" or "Having time for my garage band again."

But if you jump in without the end goal and the real reason clear in your mind, you end up with a business that takes you away from your family and friends, like my earliest jobs did. If your business preoccupations take you away from your favorite leisure pastimes, destroy your health, and let others lay claim to your time and attention, you're not doing business the right way.

And that brings me to why I wrote this book, which is to help others create more time to do the things they love. I didn't want to have to say, "My wife raised our six kids." I wanted to say, "My wife and I raised our six kids together—and it was great." So no, again, it's not about money in the first place. It's about time.

Knowing why you're creating a business will inform the way you organize that business. If you build a business right, your time should be your first consideration when you get organized. If you still believe "Time is money," think again. Time is your life back. Time gives you balance.

Ways to gain time abound: You can delegate to staff or contract out work you don't like or aren't good at. You can hire the best people out there, tell them the job, and let them do it—in your absence. You have a multitude of digital and machine automation tools for business.

Now I'm not writing a book about the ABCs of founding and operating a business. That's not my goal. Anyway, that will be your role once you know why you're in business in the first place.

I'm here to show you that if you say you're not going to retire, you're going to work till you drop, you will. You'll die right at that desk you've spent so much time at. I'm also here to show you that there's a better way, a way that balances business with your life.

We're going to be more about running a balanced life, and I'll talk about some basic business tactics only to help you achieve that. Soon you'll see that business and life become fluid.

Why a Business?

Before asking "Why *this* business?" you should ask yourself "Why business?"

Business is about making a life, not just a living. Or it should be.

Keeping your balance in the business world requires principles and practices that push for efficiencies and a set of checks and balances. If that's true (it is), why is it so? Because creating practices and efficiencies is intentional in your thrust to carve out time. Your intention is to make a rewarding, comfortable life at home, along with a prosperous business.

Life is a set of priorities, pure and simple. And one priority that appears all too extravagant when you review the vast amount of success in business books online or at a bookstore is the gleeful amount of attention paid to making money—preferably hand over fist.

Let's get any confusion here straight right now. Business is about making money. Yes, it is. No doubt about it. But it's also about making and having a life outside the business—otherwise, what was all that effort and money for? The priority that I see as off-balance is the one that imagines the endgame is how much you've earned rather than how well you've lived. The curious thing is that the best business practices I know accomplish both such that when your business does well, you can live very well too.

A business that's struggling is certainly no fun. It can and will run you ragged by the end of the day. Funny thing, though: A business that's doing terrific can run you ragged as well.

Many worker bees die in the service of their prosperous hive, and business owners do the same. They die young by not paying attention to their health. They become addicted to drugs or alcohol. They go through one, two, or more divorces. They become estranged from their children. Or they simply watch the business collapse because they've overreached or failed to put in the right checks and balances.

After some thought, it came to me that a successful, smoothly running business has a chance of allowing you to live well, not only because the revenue is solid, but because it runs on solid business practices that prevent serious frustrations and stresses from the start. Right practices don't just promote profits but do something else: They literally buy you comfort. They buy you time. They can buy you an extended life.

In short, the books that have you chasing every dollar you can get ahold of rarely consider the idea that, to live well, you'll also need time. Buying time requires implementing efficiencies, discipline, and a set of practices that together let you ride a bike, hike in the woods, go to a museum, or take a whole day off to attend a ball game with the kids.

I'll get into the details in the next chapters, but one of the goals in running a lifestyle-enhancing business is to create a franchise-like set of policies and practices for your business. In case you don't know, all franchises live and breathe rules and procedures that the franchise owner developed to run his first business. That owner turned around and said to interested franchisees, "Follow this map, and you'll succeed." If the franchisee refuses to operate by the book, they're out.

You like the concept or you don't, but one of the advantages of a franchise-style operation is everything's already been tried and tested for you. Starting your franchise means having the road map in hand without suffering through any guesswork or initial fumbling.

My book, then, focuses on key business practices that allow you to live an unfettered life. This means establishing a set of checks and balances so that when you're on that glorious fishing trip you've always dreamed about, the phone won't be ringing with someone telling you that your business is floundering without you.

Business Is Full of Distractions

No matter who you are, it's very easy to lose focus. A business that serves your lifestyle has to develop its own balance while you, as the owner, build in the protections that keep it safe.

It will be an interesting ride after you open your business. Once customers come in, a jumble of concerns spins through your mind. A short-term opportunity, a sudden surprise from a regulator, or outside forces of many kinds can turn you around quickly, and it takes only a few wrong turns to make getting back on track very tricky and time-consuming.

It will be hard to stay focused. You'll forget your goals.

In addition, your health depends on remembering your goals. You have to be willing to put in long hours at various junctures in your career, but there's a reason CEOs go out and play tennis or hit the golf course or head to Aspen in February. Your mental and physical health require leisure—quiet times when you're on call for no one.

Plan Your Living and Your Life

What I've learned with the help of some terrific books along the way is that universal questions like "What do I want my life to look like?" are best answered with a pen and paper. You can try answering them while walking along a beach, but by the time you get home, those lofty thoughts seem to evaporate into the glorious stratosphere. I want the answers in front of me, where I can see them, hold them, and check my progress from time to time. Let's see if I can help you do the same.

Planning is a daunting task for some, especially if you're tasked with planning your future happiness (life) along with the imperative of earning a living (business). You have to start somewhere, and the idea here is to start a business that serves you. So, let's write down your needs first. Then you can plan a business that answers to your needs instead of interfering with them. This is as simple as asking yourself what you want out of life and what you want out of your business.

You need a vision of what the future will bring if things go according to plan.

I'll give some suggestions to help you get started as you write down why you are starting (or started) your business, its purpose, and where you want it to take you. Exit strategies are far more important than most people realize when they start out, but the truth is the decisions you make in the first three, five, or ten years of running your business should be determined by where you want the business to end up.

My business is a prime example of this. Amata Law Office Suites is a cash flow business, not an asset-rich business, so our goal was never to own or build assets. We aimed to generate cash, which takes more discipline to protect than, say, real estate or tangible goods.

You need a vision of what the future will bring if things go according to plan. Where are you going with this business? Is it asset-based or cash flow–based?

I work with law firms every day, and there's another prime example of a cash-based business. While lawyers can certainly purchase a building for their headquarters at some point, they start out as strictly a service business with one indisputable asset: their knowledge. Their primary asset, as it happens, is themselves.

Your Pre-journey Checklist

I've said it: In business, as in life, you should focus on the journey and not expect to be parachuted to your destination. You can't exit a business with a pile of money until you've created and built the business. You can't get to a destination without taking the journey first.

Just like a checklist for your car's tire pressure, oil, wipers, and other safety issues that can make or break a road trip, there's a pre-journey checklist for starting a business. It's not what you think.

Your checklist is the set of goals on your to-do list right now—we'll stop here for a minute or two to reflect on how far you've come and where exactly you want to end up. Like many entrepreneurs, I'm goal-oriented.

I read plenty of books in my early years about how to improve your life and how to make your life a success. (There are only about a million of these books available at any given time, so go find five or six and read them!) But one of the fundamentals that hit home time and again—it must have been en vogue in the 1970s—is the value of setting goals and measuring your progress objectively.

One such story that sticks with me is the life of Jay Van Andel, who was, along with Rich DeVos, a founder of

Amway. I was only thirteen years old when I read *An Enterprising Life: An Autobiography*. With a generous spirit, Jay introduced me to the practice of asking simple, direct questions, such as "What do you want to do?" and "What do you want to achieve?" His story planted the seed that humble beginnings are not as big a disadvantage as we think. I worked with Amway distributors in my teen years, setting a pattern in which goals became plans and plans became goals. Their mentality was to put their goals in front of them as what they wanted to achieve now. Forget the past and the future. Focus on now.

In truth, that method makes me feel good about myself. There are many ways to tackle inertia or ward off those weary old blues that creep up once in a while. Setting goals is my way of countering that feeling. I have goals that cover business, health, and my mental state. I set out, for example, to read twelve books in six months, a combination of fiction and nonfiction. When I get this done, I let the achievement sink in. What did I learn? In which ways did I grow?

The simple act of reading, of paying attention to your mental health, keeps things in perspective. Absorbing new ideas reminds you that life is not a one-track endeavor, that building the business you hope will make you rich and famous is not your only goal. You want to improve your tennis game, meet new people, travel, or explore the world of opera or dance or banjo music. Yes, work remains a big time commitment, but reading reminds you that business is supposed to support you, not own you.

Putting your goals down on paper is a process. Let me guide you through some starting points and then some types of goals you should consider setting. You must (not should, but must) write them down. Here we go.

Your Accomplishments

Start by writing down what you've achieved up to this point in your life. What have you gotten good at doing? What knowledge or skills have you acquired? Maybe you've mastered Russian or you've been pretty gifted at the piano since childhood. You might know how to create mobile apps in less than a day. Whatever it is, put it on your list. Put it all in writing.

What are the positive highlights or memorable moments you've experienced? Maybe it was walking through the clouds during a mountain hike. It might be something like learning to do a full somersault off a diving board at the public pool one summer, or helping a friend get through a difficult homework assignment that you understood and they didn't.

What specific challenges have you overcome? Maybe you completely healed from a horrible injury. Maybe you're dyslexic and you were diagnosed very late in your schooling—but you overcame the obstacles it created.

That is what I mean by "accomplishments." Just start writing and get the words flowing; don't judge your list. Just write.

Now that you've examined your accomplishments, reread them and see which ones made you happy. This helps you imagine what your personal goals might be if you haven't given them much credence before.

Before goal-writing, however, it's time to take a deeper dive. Yes—next you'll write out who you are and your story.

Your Life Story

The thought of writing your life story can be overwhelming, but this is not the same as writing your autobiography. While that might be a fine idea for some, the idea here—and later, as you write out your goals—is to find out who you are. Don't get stuck just writing about your jobs or education. Write about every aspect of your life that you have strong feelings about, such as the things that are memorable, unique, empowering, or gut-wrenching.

What makes you tick? What makes you different from other people? What separates you from everybody else? What makes you happy?

These are valuable things to know. Knowing what makes you happy gives you a head start when you open a business; it helps you know how to streamline it, how to make it run more effectively and smoothly. And, if nothing else, it's the first step toward delegating, which is the first step toward running your business rather than letting your business run you.

Yes, there's a method to this writing madness. If you have no priorities other than making money, you'll be stuck at a desk day in and day out. But if you take time to review who you are and what you want out of life, you can seek a balance that keeps you healthy, wealthy, and wise.

In addition, the more you know about yourself, the easier it is to create a business that reflects your strengths, which can help you formulate the competitive advantages you can use to increase your chances of success.

Someday, when you try to explain your business to a client, a customer, an investor, a banker, or even yourself, you'll be pleased to find you can easily state what makes your business special. An idea of how your business differs from every other business out there becomes a prized selling point.

My Story

As a youth, I was very active in sports. I played baseball all summer, and then track and basketball became part of my repertoire.

Basketball was my favorite, not just for the glory and grace of the game and the fun surprises that happen when you put ten players on a small court and tell them to go at it for an hour. What I experienced playing basketball was improvement. I could measure my skills through points on the board, but also through the effort it took to run or pass or rise off the ground for a jump shot. It seemed one day I could barely run and dribble at the same time, and after some weeks went by, I could dribble without looking at the ball, flying down the court as fast as I could go. I'm right-handed, but I trained myself to dribble, pass, and shoot with my left hand only. I could see my dedication paying off.

For me, these lessons weren't transient. I could see that determination had a part to play in life, that expertise is learned. It helped me to know I could trust things to get better if I mixed desire and effort. It helped to know that general awkwardness when you start something new is part of the experience. I could therefore discount my embarrassment. One of my principal rules in life is not to fault someone for making a mistake as long as they made a decision, as long as they put in the effort to make something happen. Not trying, in my opinion, is the only true mistake in life.

And, when it came to basketball, boy, did I try. When we weren't in school, my buddies and I played every day. In the winter, we would shovel snow off a court just to play, wearing hats and sweaters if need be, exhaling puffy clouds of condensation as we ran. During the summers, we played like fiends. We were out on the court from 8:00 a.m. until it got too dark to see. Between eighth and ninth grades, I played with only my left hand to improve my chances of making the high school varsity team. By the time tryouts came around, I was completely ambidextrous on the court—a solid attribute for a high school player.

Zen and the Art of RV Travel

Later, along with going to every Cubs home game I could attend, spending time with my children, and staying healthy, I became fascinated by travel and seemed to learn about myself every time I had a chance to do so. Of course I learned about the grand, exciting world as well.

Staying curious and keeping my mind active have always been a part of my life. I'm a father, husband, businessman, athlete, and reader just trying to balance all those needs at the same time. I also think curiosity is a fundamental aspect of running a successful business. Doctors read, study, and attend seminars throughout their careers. They talk shop with their cohorts. Accountants keep up with the latest trends in their business. Human resources experts are constantly learning as well. So what if you own a pizza parlor, a gas station, or a real estate business? Constantly learning comes with the territory there as well.

Learning promotes humility. Travel also makes you humble as you confront a world that struggles and thrives almost in equal measure. Furthermore, I come from a sales background, and a healthy level of curiosity is required in that work. Why? Because in sales, there's nothing quite as valuable as listening. Being truly curious about someone else is a great reason to listen. Your customers should help define your business for you. After all, what's service all about if not giving someone something they want and perhaps can't find elsewhere?

Travel also teaches you about the transient, temporary parameters we all must face. Life is a short ride, and you can't take it with you (whatever "it" is). At some point, despite your ambitions, it comes to you that the destination is not quite the reward you envisioned, while appreciating the journey can exceed your expectations a thousandfold (I know, I know—I say this a lot).

This lesson about the journey being the big deal came to me after I purchased an RV for my family in 2012. Since then, I'm happy to say, our family has been able to travel to every US state and most of Canada. We've catalogued about twenty months of our lives on journeys enjoyed in this extravagant jalopy, sometimes outracing snails and wooly bugs and sometimes letting those speed demons outrace us. The point is we're not in a hurry, and that's our motto. We get there when we get there. Speeding to some overpriced disappointment is not our thing. Our sojourns usually average four hours of driving a day; the rest of the time, sleeping aside, we spend with books, baseball gloves and bats, Frisbees, fishing poles and bicycles, swimming trunks and horseshoe pits. We smell the roses. We recreate.

The trick is that I've never worried about my sanity while spluttering around the country in our mobile home, no matter how crowded, hot, weary, or disgruntled anyone might be. As a family, we've learned a lesson that gets me through every day: Don't sweat the destination so much. It's the journey that really counts.

I recall our earliest trips as a family when, enthused by the chance to travel and enjoy each other's company at the same time, we stopped along the journey to pick up more relatives—and we already had five kids plus my wife and me on this highway hotel. We still didn't hit our breaking point, and we managed to get everyone home healthy and relatively happy and sane.

We developed our pattern of driving a limited number of hours a day, stopping at more terrific out-of-the-way, tangent, no-name spots than you can imagine, to satisfy as many of each child's and adult's (often conflicting) interests and curiosities as possible. Any quiet park that seemed to call out for a family in need of a few hours of tossing a baseball became our turf. If a quiet stream needed some barefoot parents cooling their toes, we volunteered. If a child needed a rest from watching the world roll by, we tried to accommodate.

There were so many delicious distractions along the way that our destinations almost became moot.

Why chase after a crowded amusement park where you spend the day standing in line when you could stop at a quiet park somewhere, cook some hot dogs and hamburgers on the city-provided grill, and spend the day laughing with your family?

Yes, I enjoyed every minute of every day. We were the Barnstorming Bockstahlers! After such a journey, I explained to friends and clients how much fun we had as a family on the go with nothing to do but enjoy the ride.

Here's why I'm telling you about my family's RVing. I've hinted at this story already. This is the whole deal: Inadvertently, my RV and travel enthusiasm convinced a cohort to go out and rent an RV and take his family gallivanting around the countryside. He did just that, and a few weeks later we happened to bump into each other. I'll paraphrase how he described his trip in two words: Completely miserable.

"What went wrong? What happened?" I asked. He described a trip that was the flip side of our family's trips. Every day of his trip depended on making it to the next great destination, whatever it was. His trip turned into one sprint after another, from one over-sold destination to the next, making it a tense road race to a series of expensive disappointments. They were constantly on the clock discovering that this is a big, big country and that RVs are not designed as sprinting machines; they're made to amble, lollygag, mosey along. Nonetheless, his family dashed across the country, hating every mile that was in their way, just so they could reach an overcrowded, overpriced destination that didn't meet anyone's expectations. Their misery escalated with every passing mile. No one arrived back home happy they'd gone out in that RV.

I do hope this story of misery helps you decide what kind of business life you want to plan out for yourself. Are you racing toward a destination or enjoying a journey?

Yes, you do have to get behind the wheel and do the driving. You do have to stop for gas, check the oil, empty the sewage, and fix flat tires. Your journey won't be all water-balloon fights on a hot day and impromptu baseball games with appreciative, well-scrubbed, well-fed children. But destinations can be, in the grand scheme of things, an illusion. At the end of our lives, our biggest reward is that we don't have regrets.

Learn to appreciate the journey. And, yes, I've got a clear conscience here: I think I'm happier with a successful business, a book to read at night, and a shot at the Ironman Competition in Hawaii than I would be with half a billion dollars, two divorces, and a heart attack.

Now: Write *your* life story before we dive into your goals. Do it right now.

Write Your Personal Goals

Next come those goals. Write out goals now for your personal life—and since you've written your accomplishments and your life story to date, I hope you've been inspired by new things you want to achieve.

Personal goals can be quick accomplishments like learning to bake bread in three tries or less. Or they can be long-term aims, like earning a PhD when you have your high school diploma. Mine, as you've seen, was RVing with my family (for nearly a quarter of the eight years it took us to achieve), and we did that because it was a written goal.

Nobody is reading over your shoulder. You might have some quirky ideas of what you've always wanted to accomplish, or maybe they seem too difficult, too obscure, or too silly. Well, there's no such thing.

They say it's what you didn't get around to doing that you regret, so this list will answer that concern. If the idea of writing down goals seems new to you, your life starts now. No apologies. No hesitation.

One of my personal goals was to maintain a healthy lifestyle. I hear the medical community (not to mention my family) doesn't consider that goal silly at all. In the meantime, I've run a very successful, competitive business for the past twenty-two years in the dog-eat-dog capital of the world, Chicago, Illinois, and I've still managed to train for Ironman competitions while doing so—even after turning fifty. Now I compete in about six triathlon events per year, and two or three are full-bore Ironman races. My goal is to qualify for the annual Ironman World Championship gloriously held in spectacular Hawaii every other year, and I'm closing in on that goal every day, undeterred so far.

I could do those things because (and only because) I was intentional about my personal goals. I wrote all of them down. Always keep in mind, we can all do anything we set our minds to if we stay focused on our goals and put in the required effort to achieve them. If I can run competitively while running a competitive business, you can, too.

Put Your Personal Goals in Categories

Now, test how balanced your goals are overall with this next organizing exercise. Being balanced means applying across your life, so now write your personal goals under the appropriate category below. Did you miss any of these eight dimensions (and no, they aren't the only ones . . . keep going if you're inspired)? What would personal goals in those blank categories look like for you?

1. Physical
2. Mental/intellectual
3. Cultural
4. Emotional
5. Social
6. Vocational/educational
7. Spiritual
8. Familial

Put Your Personal Goals in a Timeline

Next, separate the goals into timelines. Which ones are for the next year, five years from now, or twenty years down the road?

As most people acknowledge, you learn to walk before you learn to run, so it helps to form short-term goals that are attainable (enroll in a four-year university) and extend them to reach your long-term goal (pursue my bachelor's, master's and then—goal!—my PhD degree).

Then the job is to find the actions you can take to get closer to each goal. Find a tangible way to put those goals into action. Under "Keep my mind sharp as long as possible," for example, write down "Read two books a month," or "Learn Spanish" or "Take two adult education courses each year." These types of additions put your goals into further focus.

Why You're Starting Your Business

Here we are—this is probably, in your mind, the destination we've been moving toward. This is when we ask why.

After all the writing I've just walked you through, you're probably better able to imagine why you want to start a business, and you might even have an idea of which one it should be to help you balance your business goals with your personal goals.

Remember, what we're looking for is a business that supports your needs, not the other way around. In fact, it's often those quirky personal goals that give people the greatest satisfaction in life. You run a marathon when you never thought you could run around the block and survive. You lose forty pounds you thought you'd be stuck with for life. Those are great goals, and you love it when you achieve them. There's nothing wrong with those at all.

Does your business concept support them? It simply has to. When you write down why you're starting your business, what its purpose is, and where you want it to take you, you're talking as much about your day-to-day work as your end goal, and also your exit strategy. This is because the decisions you make in the early years of running the business should all be guided by where you want to end up.

Now organize your business goals:

1. List them all, great and small.
2. Put them in a timeline, short term to long term.
3. Add action items that get you closer to achieving each goal.

Use Goals to Create Your Business and Life Plans

Keep all this written work you've just done within reach. Goals are your Rosetta Stone. In the effort to corral your ambitions and get what you want out of life, what's more important than creating clear goals that you can measure, appreciate, and revise when necessary?

In fact, you might find that you've known your goals all along. My business partner Frank and I both knew we wanted a business that would allow us to "do the right thing," especially when it involved the people our business supported. As one of my goals, I don't consider doing the right thing arbitrary or insignificant. It has legitimacy and requires backing up words with action.

How did that look in day-to-day work and life? I remember when one of my employees lost his eyesight and, sadly, had to step away from his job. When he gained part of his sight back, we wanted to rehire him. This wasn't possible under our insurance benefit package (it didn't allow us to make an exception in coverage for one employee). So, we changed benefits for all our employees—better coverage for the clear advantage of sleeping well at night, knowing we had done what was right.

Those are the types of goals and beliefs that idle in your subconscious. They're there all along, simmering, in a pleasant but unnoticed state. They don't always come through as coherent or tangible. Writing them down helps me transition them from abstractions to concrete commitments. That's why I said you probably knew what business you wanted to run all along; the goals you wrote down are a part of your validation and function as guideposts that help you keep your balance as you dash off into the world of commerce.

So, now, with this very important mid-journey pause and your reflections complete (because life and business are not about the destination but the journey!), let's begin the next leg of your journey: preparation of the mechanisms that will get your business off the ground. You will not have perfected your operational structure right from the start; this is your starting point. Streamlining and continuous improvement come with the territory, but for now, you have to start somewhere.

Chapter 2

Plan Your Whole Life: Define Yourself in Multiple Dimensions

Live a happy and balanced life. That's the goal (or you wouldn't have read this far). This means, among other things I'll be mentioning, separating yourself from your business.

In the thinking and writing I've guided you through, you start with the end in mind for your life. Notice that the word *business* isn't part of that. Not yet. The number one goal is to live a happy and balanced life. Just because you started your own business doesn't mean you live one-dimensionally. For example, you are not "just a lawyer." You are not just a _____ [fill in the blank with how you're tempted to introduce yourself].

If your business consumes you to the point that you're no longer spending time with your family or doing the things you love, or you're losing your health and vitality, you're living a one-dimensional life.

Your business is everything to you? That's not where you want to stay. If it's taking up all your time and you start to identify yourself through that business, you know you're in trouble. You need some separation. When COVID-19 hit, people started working from home. All of a sudden, we started working longer hours because it was easier to do. We were working from home—yay, no commute! And instead of using our former commuting time to achieve better life balance, we worked more.

That's not healthy or part of a balanced life. You need to break it out, so make time for a walk or a physical workout of some kind. That break boosts your mental and physical health. Make time to focus on your mental well-being, your physical well-being, and your emotional well-being.

Make time to have a social life outside your work; that means seeing friends who have nothing to do with your business. You won't get caught in that rut where every time you're going out, you're just talking about business—your friends are only vaguely interested anyway, so talk about them and their lives instead.

A one-dimensional life focused on business can't be sustained for long without having some kind of a negative effect on you and your home life. If you make your work fill eight, ten, or twelve hours a day, make it so for only four days a week. Plan for it, and it will happen. It happened for my family. As I've said, we bought an RV and traveled the country for twenty-two months over an eight-year period. There were weeks upon weeks when I didn't call the office. Nothing exploded. Nothing collapsed.

I know not everyone can do that, but you can take a few days every two months—whatever works for you to break away. Plan it. Write that goal down. And when it happens, shut your phone off. Why don't people want to do that? One thing I've noticed is you can't be outside playing baseball with your son, then take a phone call from work and think that won't affect your son. Plan phone-off times. Let your staff know. Put the phone on the kitchen counter and go shoot hoops and talk to your child.

Living a multidimensional life of balance calls for a plan. Be strategic about when and how you're doing things. Remember your goals.

Frank and I were in our ninth year in business. I'm a self-professed workaholic. I have no problem working twenty hours a day, but I knew that wasn't where I wanted my life to go. It wasn't why I started my company. So for me, buying the RV that year was a strategic move toward balance. It was one way to force myself to step away.

Now I set pretty lofty goals. As you've read, I'm a goals guy. Besides traveling with my wife and kids (and whoever else came along), the other thing I knew was that I had to do it while my children were young. If you're a parent, you know that as they get older, they start to have their own lives and activities that their siblings (and parents) aren't part of. So that framed our schedule to achieve this particular goal.

Don't Let Your Business Control You

Are you managing your business, or is it managing you? If it's managing you, it's just like having a salaried job and being at your employer's beck and call. If you're managing it, you can step away—you've told your staff what needs to be done, and since you hired the best you could find, they'll do it. We'll talk about this in another chapter, but hiring people and then stepping away from aspects of your business is the only way to take it to the next level of growth.

There was a program I sat through in Europe. The exercise was "Talk about everything but what you do for a living when you meet someone." It's that party game: Try introducing yourself to someone new without talking about your job, your profession, or your business at all.

To keep your balance, don't define yourself one-dimensionally.

Don't focus on that dimension of yourself for a change. What, then, will you say? Interesting, right?

American entrepreneurs have a hard time with that. We want to identify with our business/profession, but we need to step away from that. It comes back to not making yourself one-dimensional but creating a balance of dimensions instead.

Define Yourself in Six Dimensions

I've just said it: To keep your balance, don't define yourself one-dimensionally. You're not only a lawyer. You're not just a business owner. But you're also not just a parent.

How many dimensions make for work-life balance, though?

I named eight in the last chapter, just to inspire you to think of your life from those perspectives. Let's look at six of them again. These are the ones that work for me, my wife, and our family—and, I might add, my business. Look at each one and just ask, "How am I doing in that dimension?" You'll know.

1. Physical
   - Make exercise a part of your daily routine.
   - Prioritize healthcare routines and exercise the same as you would prioritize a client meeting.
   - Change up your routine occasionally to keep it fresh (and keep yourself exercising).
   - Train alone sometimes and at other times with a training partner or coach.

2.　Mental

- Relax and unwind. Take time to step away.

- Enjoy vacations without checking emails, texts, or voice messages from work.

- Resist the urge to work seven days a week.

- Find mental challenges outside work to help counter those at work.

3.　Emotional

- Take stock of how frazzled or stressed out you are.

- Follow a destress routine daily.

- Notice the quality of empathy, attention, and expression of feelings you have with family and friends.

4.　Social/leisure

- Socialize with people outside your work world.

- Prioritize time with family.

- Make time for friends.

- Make a point of meeting new people.

5. Vocational/educational

- Continuously educate yourself about new technologies and developments in your industry.
- Evaluate new tools for your work.
- Streamline processes when possible.

6. Spiritual

- Find a way to get spiritual sustenance.
- Meditate or reserve quiet time each day.
- Perhaps return to a spiritual practice or religious faith you've neglected.

Is the Prize the Journey or the Destination?

Your journey begins when you make the decision to start your business. Clearly, you're not at the destination yet.

Wrapped up in that journey is life—living in the moment and enjoying what you're doing. It's about living out a variety of dimensions daily to keep yourself balanced.

Share your success with others and become a mentor, a guide to them on their journey. Build a strong network that's as multidimensional as you are. These are people you share interests with and enjoy being around.

Driving an RV But Missing the Prize

I mentioned a client of mine who (based on my own enthusiasm) took his family to South Dakota in a rented RV. He had this prize in mind and forgot to make it about the journey rather than the destination. He forgot (or never knew, which is sadder) that the hour-by-hour, day-by-day journey is what life is. It's a journey of discovery, experiences, mistakes and successes, laughter and tears.

And, by the way, you just can't do what he did in the world of business. When you start your business, you must realize that it has to be fun. You've got to enjoy what's happening in the moment, to cherish the every-day journey. You have to end each day burning to tell someone the highlights of the day, it was that good.

Why? A lack of fun leads to burnout. You'll eventually throw in the towel. But you know business is a long game. If you want to stay in the game, it has to be fun for you.

It's just like when your kids are growing up. You don't want to miss an hour of their development. You want to cherish those days when they're in diapers, and the

"Oh, her first step! Honey, did you see that?" You have to be there because it'll never happen again. It all hits you if you're in the moment of that journey.

Running a business is that kind of journey, too. Don't go so fast and so hard that you get burned out. This is not a sprint. Maybe it's not even a marathon. Maybe it's a long walk in the park—a leisurely, delightful stroll.

We get caught up in being so busy and forget the multidimensionality of our lives and our goals. We stop achieving goals or being multidimensional humans for no reason other than we haven't made it a priority.

That takes us back to the balanced life. Make things outside of work a priority. Make going on a trip or having dinner with your family a priority. Put them on your calendar, just like you would an important meeting with a client who's going to sign that $50 million deal any minute now. Balance—and the people in your personal life—are just as important or more important than that juicy deal.

One way to think about balance is this: Ask yourself, "How many non-work items, activities, or conversations have I had today?" That's how you remind yourself to create the balanced life and live for the journey.

Part II

Mid-Journey Checklist: Business Basics for a Balanced Life

Chapter 3

Plan Your Business: Competitive Advantage

It's true that I've already put you through your paces. However, on this journey, it's now time to move from those personal considerations—all vital and part of this next adventure—to a business that serves your personal goals and helps you not only create but maintain a real-life balance.

With what you've done so far, you now know a few things that will guide you throughout your business career. The central theme here is that you know more about yourself. With this knowledge, you can plot out your business life. Let's recap:

- You've written out your personal goals and lifetime goals.
- You know what you need to keep your life functioning well on the physical, mental, emotional, social, educational, and spiritual levels.

We started with those two items because you don't want to get to the finish line and forget to enjoy life, capture the Kodak moments, celebrate your family, or take those amusing side trips that make you who you are. In short, you don't want to cross the finish line with too many regrets. Zero regrets is achievable.

I've also reminded you that because we're human, there are a lot of distractions out there. Some of those distractions will be shiny objects you're tempted to go after for your business only to discover they were counterproductive, didn't work anyway, and cost a lot. Another unnerving, time-sapping distraction we all have today is that ping on your phone. If you let it, everything from the weather to the daily news to a celebrity's new haircut to a bad driver can be very distracting. Staying focused requires vigilance, a plan of some kind (such as "I answer emails only at 11:00 a.m. and 1:00 p.m."), and discipline to stick to the plan.

To finish up our recap, you've written down your goals and put them in a drawer of your desk where you can review them from time to time, but not have them haunt you every minute of the day. You don't want to lose them, but you don't want to be nagged to death by looking for perfection, either.

And so, here we are, at the starting line to get your business up and running. What's your next step? What do you do now?

You look at your business idea to identify its competitive advantages—and I'll show you that there are more than you think.

What Sets You Apart?

If you know yourself well, you can start looking for a competitive advantage by asking what makes you and your business different from everybody else and theirs. But this is not meant to be an existential exercise. We're looking for something tangible, not esoteric.

One thing to understand here is that a business can thrive on two types of people: someone who is incredibly good at producing your business's products, and someone who is incredibly good at sales.

This is the balancing act that may require you to get a partner. Just look at Apple: It had one sales/marketing genius in Steve Jobs and one production/product genius in Steve Wozniak. Without the two skills put together, nobody would have heard of Apple Computers.

So where do you fit? Are you the master of sales or the master of production? Remember that a jack of all trades is a master of none.

What Business Will You Develop?

Do you enter a field you're familiar with, join a franchise, or find a niche that's not being serviced? You might already know because the right opportunity has already presented itself.

It's likely that your business won't be a planet-changing one but a fairly exciting option for you that others—maybe lots of others—have done before you. Don't assume most of the good ideas are already taken. The good news is you don't have to invent self-folding shirts or cure baldness in one application to make a go of it in this world.

As an example, I work in real estate development for a niche audience. It's not like I invented real estate development. It's been around for ages. My advantage is the niche audience.

We opened a company in Chicago that was essentially a commercial office development company—a realtor, basically, like tens of thousands of others. But we specialized in developing office coworking spaces only for lawyers and law firms. And that was our competitive advantage: turning an average idea into an adventurous, fun, and specific concept that has proved to be recession and pandemic-proof. While my partner Frank retired a few years ago, I'm pleased to say we continue to do very well with the business.

There are loads of pizza shops out there, but there are still brave souls ready to open a new one in your neighborhood all the time. With nearly a hundred thousand pizza parlors in the country, it pays to find a competitive edge that sets you apart from the rest. Plenty of businesses have made a killing by refashioning the ordinary and selling it as something extraordinary. Ray's Pizza in New York City sells pizza. But it was among the first to sell *gourmet* pizza, and now a quick search on Google shows there are forty-nine pizza parlors in New York called Ray's—four owned by the man who started the business (Ralph Cuomo) and forty-five copycats. There are stores in New York called Not Ray's Pizza. Really. All because Ralph Cuomo started the gourmet pizza craze. When you go to your neighborhood pizza shop and see pizza topped with asparagus, prosciutto, goat cheese, or squash blossoms, you should give a nod of thanks to Ralph of Ray's Pizza.

The thing that makes your idea "not just" is called the competitive advantage. There's still room for a fresh, enterprising face out there, whatever the service or product, ready to do battle on the open market. Therein lies a hidden truth of business.

Want to find out how you might have *multiple* competitive advantages? Take McDonald's. What does it sell? Mostly hamburgers, French fries, and soda. You can't get any more boring than that. But with thirty-eight thousand locations worldwide, the company is the absolute master of piling up the competitive advantages year after year.

It promised food cooked in less than a minute.

It guaranteed consistency, a product of the same quality every time.

Each of its locations was kept clean as a whistle.

Then there was the Big Mac. Just a hamburger? No. A burger that was taller than most, with a unique sauce. Knocked the competition out.

Over the years, there were the Happy Meal, the McFlurry, the McRib, and other items whose key marketing thrust was selling something that no one else had.

Within a few short years, there were restaurants everywhere. McDonald's used the franchise model, which helped put it "on every corner" very quickly. Another advantage. Few businesses (especially but not only business-to-consumer operations) are left in the marketplace that don't understand the beauty of franchising.

One advantage of the franchise that nobody talks about is that the store managers are often not even there. This should catch your life-balancing attention. With every task pared down to its simplest process, businesses are much more controlled and autono- mous. There are fewer unusual decisions to make.

How Will You Show Authoritative Leadership?

Narrowing your business idea down to fit a niche audience is one way to find a competitive advantage because it makes you an "authoritative leader." First, you do enough research to make sure you know what you're doing. You can't start purely by guessing. There is, of course, a learning curve for any venture. You talk to your consumers all the time (more on that is coming up) and as you learn from them, you notch a small success and move on to the next one. Each success adds to your expertise and authority in your market.

In time, guess what? You become one of the authorities in the business—the standard your competitors can only hope to rise to—and, in time, your company is the one your customer base talks about. They recommend it to friends, and your business grows and grows.

How Can You Create Competitive Advantage?

Unless you're an inventor, chances are that the type of business you've chosen has been done before. My business—except for the niche market aspect—wasn't exactly an original venture. Coworking was out there. Law firms abounded. Real estate was an age-old industry.

All that made Amata Law Office Suites a prime example of the need to create a competitive advantage out of thin air. Office real estate development has been done countless times, but specializing in offices for attorneys automatically made Amata special. And the advantages, in fact, increase over time, as I'll explain in a minute.

For now, think of something that will make your business special, even if you haven't invented a gadget no one has thought of before. All of the following classic ideas have opportunities to create a competitive advantage:

- Open a pizza parlor with any number of unique recipes or combine them with fancy craft beers. If nothing else, you can have employees who all wear funny hats or dress up for holidays or sing Italian arias.

- Open a cleaning service that's one step faster than the next or teams up with a pest control company.

- Open a bowling alley that showcases live bands on Saturday nights or teams up with a dating service where clients meet for blind-date bowling.

- Open a dance studio that offers multicultural dance, classes for people with disabilities, or performances at lunchtime in the park.

It certainly helps if you can approach your business as if it were a one-of-a-kind enterprise even if the basic formula for that business has been in place since the dawn of time. Special offerings allow your business to build a reputation as a special kind of company. You can reap a few of the benefits that niche businesses garner. Here are some niche business benefits to think about:

- By creating a business that is not often or easily replicated, you eliminate much of your competition right from the start. This is called a "high barrier to entry," and you create the barrier.

- While you start out as a specialist or become one, you will be able to raise prices based on your expertise. Higher prices are associated with higher quality in people's minds.

- As time passes, you become known by customers who recommend you as the business that caters strictly to specific needs. You are The One who provides that rare service.

During downturns, many businesses find they have to cut prices or refrain from raising them. If you truly design a niche business and develop valuable skills and authority, you could not only survive a downturn but avoid fear of raising prices. After all, if you're the best at what you do or the only one around who does it, you can just about name your price.

Like with any business, do your research first.

Like with any business, do your research first. Amata Law Office Suites relies on its identity of catering to lawyers as a competitive advantage to the point that we are defined as a niche business. We don't do other types of commercial space plus attorneys. None. Never. We focus only on attorneys and only, thus far, in the Chicago area. It's very, very niched—even though in 2022, there were 57,262 lawyers practicing in Chicago alone (and that sounds like a lot).[1] This means, more than likely, a lot of desks, office chairs, reception spaces, conference rooms, and snack areas were in order. One online source I noticed recently said there was so much corruption in the city that lawyers in Chicago are never out of work. While that's good for us, we hope that sentiment is a bit tongue-in-cheek. Nonetheless, you can read between the lines: It pays to find your competitive advantage, whether it's a specialty market, a low price only you can honor

---

1   Mary F. Andreoni, *2022 Annual Report of the Attorney Registration and Disciplinary Commission of Illinois* (ARDC, 2023), https://www.iardc.org/Files/AnnualReports/AnnualReport2022.pdf.

(and still make a profit), or a service done in a manner no one else does.

How Can You Achieve Brand Recognition?

McDonald's. Coca-Cola. Starbucks. Why do you know these names? These companies keep them in front of their consumers to establish brand recognition. That means when a consumer wants a burger, a soda, or a coffee—what do they think of? Of course.

Everything your business does reminds your target clients of you, your logo, your tagline, and your photo in the ads (or whatever you do to brand yourself and the business). That's your competitive advantage over all the others out there who are selling what you offer.

What's Your Niche?

What services or products can you provide with a competitive advantage?

This is an interesting one. You either know what business you want to start because you're going to be doing the same thing you've been doing, or you'll step outside your comfort zone, based on previous work, and start a business you're less familiar with.

Outsourcing was my business before Frank and I started Amata. We thought we could probably get around our noncompete by going after some companies that outsourced and taking over their operations. That was how we started because it was what we knew very well. The problem was that I ended up getting sued by my previous employer, and that lawsuit cost me $250,000. So it wasn't necessarily the right way to go. All I'll say is beware of past agreements you've signed and respect them.

Start a business doing something you know very well in which you can create a niche that's hard for anyone else to duplicate. That's your competitive advantage, and frankly, I see so many entrepreneurs without that competitive advantage—they're not putting it out there in front of their market. For example, if you open a plumbing or electric services business, remember how many of these are out there. What's your twist? What makes you different? A good friend of mine started an HVAC business and then added plumbing to it. A plumber, in the earliest days of solar, added solar system installation to the company's services (when there were really no nationwide companies doing this). That HVAC expert and that plumber established authority. They were the forerunners in their field, the go-to providers, and they made themselves memorable through in-your-face branding, piling up the competitive advantages very smartly.

As for Amata, we're the only one offering our palette of services solely to attorneys, so attorneys think, "The team at Amata know us. We like that. Call 'em up."

How can you make yourself unique? And what competitive advantage(s) can you put forward?

How Can You Provide Great Customer Service?

The one thing that always sets you apart—and that's falling apart in our country—is great customer service. If you haven't read the book that describes the Walt Disney Company's training and customer service processes, you should. It's titled *Be Our Guest: Perfecting the Art of Customer Service*.[2]

When you walk through Disney parks or hotels, you never see trash. Part of their idea of customer service is cleanliness. It's a comprehensive program, and they swear by it. The training and development of their people are outstanding.

How can you make sure your customer service is the best in the market? Hint: It might just be a matter of noting what's awful about the customer service at your top competitors' businesses. The truth is your clients

---

2   Disney Institute with Theodore Kinni, *Be Our Guest: Perfecting the Art of Customer Service* (Disney Editions, 2011).

won't leave you if you have great customer service—however, if you fail at it, they will (and in a heartbeat).

Disney and other great companies train to provide great customer service. They do the training for more than one reason, in fact:

- Companies with comprehensive employee training programs have 218 percent higher income per employee than those without such programs.
- A global survey found that companies are 17 percent more productive and 21 percent more profitable when they offer training to engaged employees.
- Businesses that invest in employee training see a 24 percent higher profit margin overall.[3]

Great customer service is taking care of people and making every interaction with you an amazing, awesome experience. Developing that competitive edge is what keeps people coming back and recommending you to others.

You can't let yourself get complacent in a business. Make sure your business always puts customer

---

3   Devlin Peck, "Employee Training Statistics, Trends, and Data in 2024," Devlin Peck, January 10, 2024, https://www.devlinpeck.com/content/employee-training-statistics.

service first. When you develop a competitive advantage, baby it. Nurture it. Put it out there in a consistent
manner. Communicate it loud and clear. Consumers
don't forget.

Chapter 4

Plan Your Business: Revenue Generation vs. Cash Flow

Those statistics about training I slid into the last section should have whetted your appetite for ways to generate efficiencies, sales, and greater profits for your new business. You'll need that. But here, it's going to be all about understanding two aspects of money: cash flow and revenue generation. Let's go old-school. Here's what Investopedia says about these two:

- Cash flow is the net amount of cash being transferred into and out of a company.

- Revenue is the money a company earns from the sale of its products and services.[4]

Cash Flow Is the Biggest Deal

Cash flow is what keeps your business alive day-to-day and week to week. It's money on hand (in your bank account) that you can spend as needed on bills, payroll, vendor services, equipment repair, etc.

With that in mind, the last thing you need to do is spend money unwisely, but using cash from your bank account is much thriftier than using a line of credit that requires interest payments. Cash flow is pure gold— and you should always be miserly about your gold.

However, this means when you sit down and calculate how much revenue you expect from your business, remember that cash flow is more useful than revenue. Even though you logged that revenue on paper, there are some caveats:

- Some clients don't pay on time.
- Some clients tear up their contracts or leave town in a hurry.
- Some go broke.

4   J. B. Maverick, "How Are Cash Flow and Revenue Different?," Investopedia, May 14, 2024, https://www.investopedia.com/ask/answers/011315/what-difference-between-cash-flow-and-revenue.asp.

- Some try to negotiate a lower rate after the service or product is provided.

This means the revenue that indicates the worth of all your contracts might not accurately reflect the cash you have to pay off a debt or take on a new risk.

Cash flow helps you survive the unexpected, and the unexpected is one of the few guarantees in life. Do you want examples? In 2006, the Great Recession began to form like a hurricane down in the tropics. By 2008, it was barreling up the coast, so to speak, but those who read the great economic journals of the day—top newspapers and magazines—found that almost none of the wizards of Wall Street or Washington, DC, saw it coming at all.

This ended up being the second-largest economic downturn in US history in a country with 15,640 economists in it (according to the US Department of Labor) and maybe one or two noticed it before it hit. This is the equivalent of a massive hurricane completely unnoticed by America's 4,874 meteorologists (I looked that up, too).

The second obvious example is the COVID-19 pandemic. Bam! In a single day, the entire economy ground to a halt, and it stayed in that limbo for months. And not just this country but the world. Who saw *that* coming? (I won't ask about public health officials, much less those disgraced economists.) And who knew how long the country would be shut down? One hotel owner, maybe.

Large and small changes in your market are a given in the business community. The United States and much of the globe recently faced a startling rate of inflation. Every business in the world had to make changes accordingly, and the one clear protection they had that cost very little was their cash flow. Those who have to react by borrowing money are, in effect, shooting themselves in the foot.

You might be lured into believing you need "real money" only in your start-up phase. Not so. There are several junctures at which your business will need to have plenty of extra cash on hand. Here are some examples:

- When a prized asset comes along and you feel it offers you a pricing advantage or a worthwhile increase in sales. If it's a prize, the seller will only give it up for cold, hard cash.

- When you want to expand because more inventory, more advertising, more staff, and the latest tech upgrades will all cost you money *before* those new sales start rolling in.

- When the company van or that workhorse HP printer gives up the ghost and needs replaced.

You nailed it, though: You'll need extra cash when you're just starting up. While you're waiting for the revenue stream to grow from an occasional drop to a steady trickle to a strong, predictable flow, you'll find the need for extra cash is knocking on your door.

Entrepreneurs have to make decisions even when expectations or anxiety is heightened.

What do you need it for? Rent. Initial marketing and advertising. Those first few hires or freelance contractors. The computers you were happy to buy that suddenly require expensive software. And on and on.

It's a scary, exhilarating time. And, as I'll point out from time to time, both of those feelings are very dangerous.

Entrepreneurs have to make decisions even when expectations or anxiety is heightened (they often occur at the same time). You'll need to practice financial discipline, one of the pillars of creating a business that doesn't collapse or implode or drive you to drinking. In this case, "no better time than the present" is not good enough when it comes to financial discipline. You have to plan your finances out yesterday, before you get started, not today, in the heat of battle.

It's often said you need a six-month cushion before you start your business, because even long-lived giants like Coca-Cola had to catch on before their potential became reality. Maybe you've invented shoelaces that never come undone until you speak a magic word. Everyone will want those, but it will still take a long time before everyone knows that.

How much cash padding will be enough? Maybe the trick is to ask yourself how long the average business in your field lasts before calling it quits. Yes, I waited with this bad news. I didn't want to see you throw my book under a moving freight train just yet. But here it is: About one in five businesses fail in the first year, and only a quarter make it past fifteen years.[5] About 82 percent of small/new businesses fail due to cash flow problems (not enough ready cash).[6]

---

5   Since 1994, the highest rate of first-year failures is 21 percent. Bureau of Labor Statistics, "Total Private: Table 7. Survival of Private-Sector Establishments by Opening Year," 2023, https://www.bls.gov/bdm/bdmage.html.

6   "Closing Strong: Year-End Cash Flow Strategies, Monitoring, and the Role of Spend Management Platforms," U.S. Bank, November 16, 2023, https://spend.usbank.com/blog/closing-strong-year-end-cash-flow-strategies-monitoring-and-the-role-of-spend-management-platforms.

Now, go back up to the top of the chapter and read it again. Yes, cash flow is that important. What did you think the phrase "Follow the money" meant? This is it.

One way to avoid cash flow problems is not to spend until you're forced to. We'll get into this more in the finance section, but you must be prepared.

A lot of law firms start their business by going out to lease nice office space. They spend too much on furniture and technology. They don't think through how much cash flow they need to survive because they won't have clients paying them from day one, but if they're lucky, they'll get payments starting about sixty days in. That first month, maybe the first six months, they need enough cash flow to survive until their first billings begin to flow in.

I imagine most businesses are the same way. You won't have revenues coming in your first day. Or, if you do, it won't be enough. Get help making a budget. It's a strong start.

Revenue Generation

When you sit down to plan your business, you'll likely need a calculator and the help of an accountant. You'll want to know what revenue to expect—money earned from product and service sales, plus whatever you earn from investments.

Revenue, as I've said, turns out to be a number in a ledger. It's certainly an indicator of the health of a company because, all things being equal, if your expenses remain the same and your revenue drops, you might have a problem on your hands. Conversely, when expenses remain low and revenue rises, you're sitting pretty—but you still need to set aside lots of cash.

I hope you're getting this (whether you understand the basics of accounting or not): On a day-to-day basis, revenue is not the same as cash flow. You'll need cash to pay off debts, fund expansion, or provide security against future challenges.

You Need a P&L

What else do you need? We'll get more into this later, but every business needs an annual profit-and-loss (P&L) statement. In the early days, you need it monthly. Without it, all those expenses, from random and unexpected ones to consistent and predicted ones, are tallied up and matched to your various revenue streams. Better to make $110,000 in a year over $100,000 in investment/expenditures than to make, say, $90,000 or $95,000. When you're up to your earlobes in business decisions day in and day out, it's hard to be objective, so the P&L will tell you if a service or product is bleeding cash so you can discontinue it, raise its price, or modify it (and test its profitability again). Or it will tell you when you're sitting pretty with a profitable service or product. If you don't know, you can't make proper decisions.

Developing Your Revenue Model
You don't have a business without sales. That's the name of the game: It all starts with selling. But you must have a way to get that sales revenue in the door.

There are revenue models for businesses, ways to be paid that you can adopt and adapt. As examples, here are four common revenue models:

1. Consumers purchase from you and pay in full up front (retail and online sales).

2. Clients sign up for your subscription services and pay every month for them (maintenance contracts for vehicles, insurance premiums, online trade publications, etc.). Or you give them a discount for buying a year's subscription in advance (the money's in your bank account right away).

3. A client orders services, and you agree the client pays one-third to start work, one-third midway through the job, and the final third upon completion (construction jobs).

4. The client pays an amount up front, called a retainer, and you bill real-time hours worked and expenses against the retainer (attorneys and private investigators do this).

Your chosen revenue model is how you'll collect that money. If you're not collecting money, your business will fail. If you're collecting money, but it's not enough because you've priced yourself too low, your business will struggle or fail too.

Part of your revenue model might be the upsell. Once you have a client, it's so much easier to make more money from that client by selling them additional services or products than it is to go out and hunt for a brand-new client.

I can use my company to illustrate this. As I write this in 2024, Amata has right around 1,200 contract clients. If they have an office space with us, it's easier to get that client to use our phone services and our paralegal services (any additional services, in fact) than to go beat the bushes for a new client. It's easier for us to incrementally increase our revenues that way. We call that "picking the low-hanging fruit."

If you're an attorney with a solo practice, you wear at least three hats: one to go out and pick up brand-new clients, one to do the work you just sold, and another to build the relationships with your existing clients that will continue to provide you new or upsell business. After their initial purchase is complete, you want to stay in touch with them (and I'll give you ways to do that in the next chapter) so that their first instinct is to reach out to you because they perceive you as their go-to attorney. You are their main point of contact for anything in the legal realm. This generates new revenue for you from your current clients. So you must look at a current client not as a one-time revenue source but as a residual revenue generator.

Computer service companies use my model: You pay monthly retainers for their maintenance service availability (maybe 24/7/365), but when your accountant spills coffee all over her keyboard or whatever, who do you buy a new one from? Right! From the same computer service company you already call all the time because it's top of mind. Even if it doesn't sell hardware, it's the first company you call.

In Amata's revenue model, when we first opened our doors, the majority of our business was going to be recurring—a blend of the retainer and subscription models. We would sign clients to licensing agreements for twelve to thirty-six months, paid every month. No *re*selling them for up to three years. However, we would *up*sell them (add on services for a new fee) over that time. Low-hanging fruit.

And speaking of low-hanging fruit, you can stay connected to your current clients in a number of ways. That's next.

Chapter 5

Plan Your Client Communication Strategy

Let me remind you why you should stay in touch with people who are already clients, customers, or consumers of your products or services. You can upsell or resell to them and get referrals from them. But it's also a matter of doing the right thing. As Frank used to say, you should do it to make sure you're doing the right thing by them and by your business.

I hear you say, "Ron, Ron. You mean *me? I* have to communicate with my customers? That's the silliest thing I've ever heard. Waste of time. My marketing people are good. That's *their* job."

Most business owners don't do the communication thing very well. Let's get into the weeds on that. There are, I believe, twelve reasons you should stay in touch with those who have bought something from your business.

1. Stay Top of Mind with Them

Whatever your revenue model, product, or service, you need to be in touch with clients regularly and frequently—and not just when something's gone wrong. You want to make sure you're giving them their expected service, or you'll risk losing them. When current clients leave you, that's leakage.

How should you do this regular and frequent communication? Clients like phone calls. They like to be talked to in person (and believe me on this: The more automated services become, the more people seek out human connection). They like that you're in touch when nothing's wrong.

A happy client tells no one. An upset client tells twelve people.

We all call clients when something's wrong, or at least we should. Maybe they complained about something. Maybe they give us a notice to terminate our services or just leave. They'll tell you they're unhappy. One day they just stop coming back to you. And more importantly, they might tell other people not to work with you.

It's the old adage: A happy client tells no one. An upset client tells twelve people (who tell twelve more people . . .).

Constantly talking to your clients can happen in other ways. We've found success with surveys starting, say, ninety days after someone becomes a client, then semiannually. We ask about services they're receiving, services they would like to see, or problems they have that we may be able to assist them with. This is also how we find out about a new service we could roll out that would help them. We reach out to clients and schedule meetings to talk about their business: what's changing and what's coming up for them. This gives us the opportunity to talk about services we're rolling out.

Remember, this regular and frequent contact happens in good weather and bad. It's not always just to hear or discuss things that are going wrong. They might reveal a great client experience, so we ask them to give testimonials on their website and on ours. It's also a great opportunity to ask for referrals and multiply the opportunities one contact offers.

At Amata, we realize they're using us and staying with us because of trust. We extend that trust to get them to start using our paralegals and our legal admins and our court filers. When clients already have trust in what you do and how you do it, it's so much easier to build your business.

2. Harvest Good Ideas

Linked to what I just said about seizing opportunities, one of our clients mentioned a service they would like to have: paralegal support. We just took their idea and gave it to them. Today, paralegal services represent 25 percent of our revenues and are a growing profit center for us. This very substantial outcome arose from a simple, relaxed sit-down conversation with one client.

It started when they asked us, "Hey, do you have someone who can do this?" We didn't at the time, but we knew how to find someone. We started hiring people and had no problem keeping them busy.

Don't wait for the client to ask. The simple question "What problem do you have now that you can't solve?" can bring that prickly problem to their mind and, who knows? Maybe it's something you can solve for them. If you don't ask, you'll never know.

3. Remind Them of How You're Serving Them

This is a quarterly review with your client. You might send out an invitation allowing them to select the date and time. Then you send them back an agenda for the quarterly review. That gives you the opportunity to tell the client what business has been done over the past ninety days. You can provide statistics for the services you've provided them and whatever else you and they have put on the agenda. It's a great tool for continuously illustrating to them why they're paying you. And when you're doing those quarterly meetings, the client has the opportunity to appreciate your efforts, ask questions, and understand why they're paying you that fee.

As an example, my tax advisors do this. They use the review meeting to state what they've done for me since our last meeting. They then use the time to find out what has changed in my and my company's situation that they can help with.

I can use one of our virtual clients as another great example. They've been paying us a fee of $200 a month for the last ten years. Loyal client, right? At some point they might ask themselves, *Why do I keep paying out this money?* Here's why: We're always in front of them at that regular review meeting, explaining why they're paying us $200 a month, $2,400 a year. We're reminding them of the benefits they're getting. We're involving them in our business by asking them, "What problem are you having trouble solving? Can we help?" And it works—they've been with us for a decade.

4. Get Ahead of Complaints

It pays off when you respect your clients by just listening, because you pay more attention to what they say. A good salesman has a great pitch, but an even better salesman listens to their clients as well. So first, we listen. I've found listening to your client's expectations and needs helps you get it right.

Beyond getting it right, it's always nice when you can exceed expectations rather than simply matching a need. When you do this, clients believe they're in the hands of a specialist. You're supposed to know your business better than your competition, better than anyone, clients included. When you impress a client that much, you gain their respect.

You need to be in touch with clients quite often to make sure you're giving them the service they're paying for, or you'll lose them. When you onboard a client, a lot can go wrong because it's usually a multistep process. If you're not in constant communication during onboarding and immediately afterward, you might miss something. You can't make sure the experience they had was what they expected or better. If onboarding was bumpy and you didn't do something to change that perception, you could lose the client.

After onboarding, you want to communicate to make sure they're happy with onboarding. If they did have negative experiences, you want to be able to understand why and immediately fix them. You might fix the problems either by giving a credit, explaining what happened so that they understand, or doing something else that shows the client you're sorry and they're very important to you. You want them to walk away with a positive experience. Many business owners don't think about this.

Some businesses have intake processes. Construction operations, law firms, moving companies, realtors— they sit with you or talk on the phone with you to ask questions and listen. They explain their services up front to prevent misunderstandings (and later complaints). Part of that might be signing a detailed service contract.

You still need to be following up with the client. Your employees may tell you that everything went wonderful, no issues, perfect. But then you talk to that client, who shakes his head and tells you, "Boy, it was pretty slow. I didn't get a good response. They didn't ask me about _____ like I expected." That client's perception is different from your employee's perception. Your strategy must be to get that from the client directly in a conversation with them.

Yes, the internet has changed the game because a single disgruntled client can write reviews that go viral—for or against you. You need to address the complaint. You may not be able to respond to everyone, but you can make sure you and your staff do the right thing.

You don't need to dig too deep to understand what the right thing is. That doesn't mean giving away the shop, just providing good customer service. If you have a culture of great customer service (and use the twelve communication tactics in this chapter), not many complaints will arise.

5. Keep a Customer Service Mindset

Bain & Company found that companies with a customer experience mindset drive revenue 4–8 percent higher than the rest of their market.[7] I believe that. I believe simply having a mindset or a culture of great customer service will drive more consumers to you and generate more revenue for you. Face it: Not a lot of companies (or industries) have high profit margins, and if yours is one of those low-margin ones, 4–8 percent more profit will skyrocket you to the top of the list.

This goes back to the Disney mindset of taking care of your customers and training your employees to do it well. The mindset that all your employees should have is not *Oh crap, the phone keeps ringing off the hook*. Instead, they should be focused on how politely and professionally they talk to clients on the phone, over live chats on the web, or via email. We do so much communication on the internet and the phone. The words you say should be in a written script, and for many call centers, this is the rule. When you write out automated responses, you think about how clients will understand them.

A great example happened to my company Amata. We do call intake for law firms in which we take messages,

---

7   Frédéric Debruyne and Andreas Dullweber, "The Five Disciplines of Customer Experience Leaders," Bain & Company, April 8, 2015, https://www.bain.com/insights/the-five-disciplines-of-customer-experience-leaders.

then communicate their content in a form that often goes out in an email. We had one client who wasn't receiving his emails, and none of us knew why. We did a little research and found the messages were hung up in the server. This client had around forty-six email messages that got hung up, and he clearly didn't get to them in a timely fashion.

Had this happened to any other client? We didn't know. So we had a big team meeting. We decided to call every client who used that service (over two hundred of them) and tell them what happened, explain what we'd done to fix it, and even apologize in advance if they suddenly got a whole list of messages at once.

Here's the communication strategy: *Never* wait for the complaint call to come in to take action. We were proactive because we understand how often a client won't call to complain; they'll just end up leaving you.

Another aspect of the proactive call strategy: We chatted with them, and it turned out we actually added business by making those phone calls. They were all happy to chat and hear that we'd addressed whatever the issue was even though it hadn't affected them.

This is just one great example of how reaching out to talk to the client pulls all sorts of benefits together.

6. Contact Your Clients for Serendipity

Here's how a "serendipity call" looks (and by the way, it was intentional on the supplier's part; it was serendipitous for me).

Amata has a furniture vendor. We're getting ready to furnish another twenty-thousand-square-foot facility. I had a different furniture vendor reach out to me—one I didn't know about and therefore wouldn't have used—and instead of giving a hard sales pitch, he invited me to a social event. I expected the hard sell (that was the sales guy in me), but it didn't happen. Since then, though, he's invented reasons to call me a couple of times.

Now he's one of the suppliers on our list for this new space; to him it's a potential $350,000 deal. He created a reason to call me that was not a hard pitch but was one I had interest in. That led to us talking and him having (from no chance at all) an opportunity to secure that piece of business. There was *never* a hard-sell moment with this supplier, and you know what? I think that's exactly what sold me.

7. Contact Your Clients When They Leave

Why is it important to survey, call, and talk to clients who are leaving? The answer is *not* "To keep them from leaving." That would be great, but it's not realistic.

Here's a better reason: If you can have an honest conversation with them as to why they're leaving, it might be a learning opportunity for you and your people—a chance to spot an issue with your operations or procedures (or procedures you don't have but should). In other words, you might just be informed about a problem that needs fixing in your business.

But even more importantly, your last interaction with them needs to be positive. I've lost clients with whom I've had very positive exit interviews; two years later, they come back to work with me again. I'm convinced it was because the exit interview was a positive experience for them. They left with a positive mental image of me and my company and remembered it when they were in the market again.

8. Contact Your Clients to Learn and Retrain Your Staff

This is really about listening to clients who contact you as well as those you contact. It's also about not being afraid of failure, learning from your mistakes, training, and brainstorming for incremental improvement.

When your staff hears a client complaint in the course of their work, do they just sweep it under the rug and not even mention it or make any note of it? When your staff hears a client suggestion, do they also think, *Nice!* and forget to make a note?

How do you ever find out? If you're lucky, you bring it up yourself by chance, only to learn that two of your staff heard this complaint and never mentioned it. Ask them why, and you'll often find they just didn't think it was important.

Any complaint, request, or suggestion from a client is important. You set the tone here as the business owner. All staff need to know it's good to report complaints and suggestions they hear from your clients. At Amata, we use Planner in Office 365 to make sharing such notes easy (and all staff can see the note), so that no feedback—whether it's a big deal or just a "little thing the client mentioned"—slips through the cracks.

Kaizen is a reason to make such notes. It's a Japanese term for an American concept that means a good change or improvement. It's about making small, incremental changes every day that snowball into significant improvements over time.

I don't look for a 20 percent improvement in my business today. But can we make a one percent improvement day after day? Terrific. Make these little improvements all the time, and you'll see great growth in your operational efficiency and your bottom line.

Let's be honest: The ones that are affecting your clients the most are your frontline employees. They need to be giving you input about how to improve those client touches so that you can improve your overall customer experience. Put something like Planner in place to become aware of what your frontline employees are seeing. The more they note the major feedback and especially the small comments they hear, the faster you'll see patterns to act on. Almost all communication is a long game, and it's good when you start seeing patterns over time and can act on what they're telling you.

Your staff will start to understand what you always knew: They're a part of the solution or a part of coming up with that solution. They have ownership, they have buy-in, and they're going to work really hard to make their part of the business (and thus, the whole business) successful.

9. Contact Your Clients a Dozen Times a Month

The frequency of communication with your current clients needs to be tracked somehow. Automate it and train staff to use the tool. Make it okay to use it for both brief contact and longer discussions. Make it record both ways—times when the client called you and when you called the client.

Use all the ways I talk about above to be in touch—but keep a record so that you know whether your goal of a dozen touches has been reached, and how.

10. Contact Your Clients in a Way That Speaks to Them

Every business is a people business and a relationship business. That implies that the better you understand what makes people tick, the better you can get along with them and predict their needs, right?

Amata started using a product called Crystal Knows. If you're familiar with the older DISC Assessments, the goal is the same for both tools: identifying someone's personality type. Assessments from these tools give you hints about things to say and ways to say them so you can cater more directly to their personality.

Note that this is never about manipulating them, just forming a more authentic connection.

We had a client whom I couldn't understand, quite honestly. I struggled with her because I'm more of a direct "This is what I've got" type of person, and she's more of a "How does that fit in my rulebook?" type of person. Using Crystal Knows gave me that *aha!* moment about her. Since then, I've changed my entire communication style to something closer to the way she's comfortable talking and working. It's on you to adapt, and we all have to do it to some extent.

I have my team using this technology. Before they make a call or send an email to a prospect or client, they go to Crystal Knows. The tool looks the client up on LinkedIn and elsewhere online to create a profile explaining the most effective ways to communicate with them. It's 80 percent spot-on in our experience, and it's pretty close on the other 20 percent. It makes my team feel like mind-readers.

I tried this with the client I just mentioned and got an immediate response, whereas in the history of our calls together, I never got a response.

11. Contact Your Clients to Keep Your Ear to the Ground

Your ability to run an agile or responsive business depends on your ability to communicate. You need to be able to communicate with all the people involved in your operations, but most of all, you need to communicate with your clients and prospects.

Some business owners never seem to get around to this. You must, or you'll miss out on some easy sales. You'll risk your cash flow and even your business.

You can't do this on your own. You have to be communicating all the time with clients, prospective clients, leads, people in your business network, vendors—all of whom can help you find success or streamline efficiencies. You absolutely have to talk to your employees and encourage them to come to you with client feedback and operational issues—they're the ones who have their feet and ears on the ground. Who better to give you the play by play or the score?

I'm old-school, having started my career in sales. Therefore, I believe communication is mostly code for listening. Asking questions and listening, unless you're a politician or a preacher, is the whole ball of wax when you're communicating with anyone. Only confident businesses ask, "What do you think we're doing right—or wrong? Let us know." You want to be able to adapt quickly and seize opportunities before others beat you to it, so you have to keep your ears and eyes open 24/7.

One story that illustrates the need to communicate through listening, asking probing questions, and collecting information comes from a racial bias complaint I recently fielded from a client of ours—a hard one at first glance. I had to make the call to answer this client's concerns, and believe me when I say there was a knot in my stomach. I was personally shocked and professionally shaken by this kind of situation arising from my work. My voice, I believe, cracked at the beginning of this phone call, but my discomfort was quickly replaced with my humanistic concern and my client's generosity in sharing his story. We reached a mutually safe and respectful place in due course, but my one overriding sensation was the realization that communicating, for better or worse, for whatever it's worth, is a failure only if you don't try.

This client and I built confidence in each other as a result of our efforts. I thought it was going to be a tough phone call. The hardest part, as it turned out, was just dialing the phone. After that, the call was worth more than I can put into words.

I would go as far as to say if you don't like talking with your clients, it may be a sign you're in the wrong business. Besides, as if it weren't obvious enough, studies have shown again and again that customer service is a profitable business practice.

If you weren't impressed by my earlier data proving why you should have a customer communication strategy, here's more:

- PricewaterhouseCoopers sponsored research that found 86 percent of buyers are willing to pay more for the same product backed with great customer service.[8]

- A TCN survey found 70 percent of people prefer customer service by phone and 40 percent view "multiple options for communicating" as the most important customer service feature.[9]

- Zendesk found half of consumers would stop working with a company after just one bad customer service experience, and four out of five would go with a competitor after two bad experiences.[10]

- Keeping customers from leaving you by providing great customer service is one of the most effective ways to make more money.

---

8   Mike Farrell, "PwC: Consumers Will Pay More for Better Experience," *NextTV Multichannel News*, March 27, 2018, https://www.nexttv.com/news/pwc-consumers-will-pay-more-better-experience-418882.

9   "TCN Consumer Survey Finds Americans Overwhelmingly Prefer to Interact with a Live Person When Dealing with Customer Service Reps," *Business Wire*, July 27, 2021, https://www.businesswire.com/news/home/20210727005281/en/TCN-Consumer-Survey-Finds-Americans-Overwhelmingly-Prefer-to-Interact-with-a-Live-Person-When-Dealing-with-Customer-Service-Reps.

10   *Zendesk Customer Experience Trends Report 2020*, accessed September 26, 2024, https://www.zendesk.com/blog/zendesk-customer-experience-trends-report-2020.

According to Bain & Company, a tiny increase in customer retention—just 5 percent—leads to a profit boost of more than 25 percent.[11]

12. Contact Your Clients Using a System

Let's just sum up here: Communication is so critical and so often taken for granted that it deserves an internal process that you require your staff to follow. The culture of communication starts in your job descriptions and materializes through a repeatable, written process everyone is trained on and expected to adhere to.

Training should start with a reminder that bad news travels faster than good news. Thanks, internet! Social media and review sites can make a single piece of bad news go viral in minutes, whether it's true or not. Everyone needs to pay attention to the application of your communication processes. Coach your staff in team meetings. Praise those who have followed the process and had successes.

The goal of good communication policies is to tell you how fast to get ahead of bad news and (if it's too late) how to address it. The negative repercussions of failing to respond to a complaint seem obvious—but what is

11   Amy Gallo, "The Value of Keeping the Right Customers," *Harvard Business Review*, October 29, 2014, https://hbr.org/2014/10/the-value-of-keeping-the-right-customers.

your internal process for doing that? If a perfectly good marriage can go sour when communication stops, just imagine what it can do to a business, in which it's an uphill trip the entire way (with competition always nipping at your heels).

I recommend starting to design the client communication system for your business before you even open. It doesn't have to be fancy: Technology has changed the communication game, but old-school methods are still allowed and often yield great surprises. The rule can simply be to pick up the phone and call a customer instead of emailing or texting them. Visiting customers where they work is an example of old-school connecting. Your system might include a standard way to answer the phone or greet customers in person. It might also include introducing yourself with a full name and title, not just "Hi, I'm Brandie."

If this sounds like it comes from an old-school salesman, yes, it does. I may be just a bit particular when it comes to communication. To me, communication is sales. Sales is essentially half of any business concern, the necessary sibling to services or production. And behind the idea of sales is the idea of customer service. Behind customer service is just plain talking to people.

In my sales-oriented world, I frequently use the word *touch* to refer to any opportunity I can find to communicate with a customer. With either a business-to-customer or business-to-business company, close contact with your clients is essential. It's so important that even an honest gesture to communicate can firm up the foundation under a shaky business deal. Customers see every effort to communicate as a goodwill attempt, and they appreciate it.

Don't be concerned if you have to fabricate a reason to get in touch with your clients. We send out a semi-annual survey just to stay in touch. We have a regular check-in for all customers ninety days after they've signed up to do business with us. We also build a culture of communication so that every incidental interaction with a client can be a valuable opportunity to engage in the two most important aspects of communication: asking questions and listening.

Communication and sales are constants—we seize every chance to discuss with clients any new services we're rolling out. The client may not need this new service today. But they may need it sometime in the future, or they may have lunch that week with someone else who does.

Moreover, change is always right around the corner, and staying in touch with both major and occasional customers can be a way to stay ahead of the competition or to turn on a dime during lulls in business (pandemic shutdowns, anyone?). Communication with clients is what led us to develop our paralegal services. It was a client's request. We sat in a huddle at our offices, brainstormed about it, and embraced it. That service now represents a quarter of Amata's revenues. What are the possibilities for your business?

Keeping your ear to the ground when demand is steady, supplies are within reach and affordable, and the rules of the game seem stable is vital to avoiding surprises. Every business has had to adapt to at least one disruptive change in its industry, or to technology, or just to people who used to buy a certain way and don't anymore. We also know that providing attentive, professional, timely service to the purchaser is often as important as ensuring the product's quality. I spoke about this in chapter 3. But just to pound my point one more time, studies show this to be true. In research from Salesforce, 80 percent of respondents said the customer service experience was just as important as the products or services they were looking to buy.[12] In other words, excellent service is important to

---

[12]   Salesforce Research, *State of the Connected Customer Report*, 6th ed. (Salesforce, 2023).

customers, so it needs to be important to you if you want to win them over.

Yes, some of the complaints you receive are going to be serious, but the value and promptness of your communication and your willingness to listen will earn you benefits at the end of the day.

Chapter 6

Process Management: Operations and Technology

You need to move quickly (before day one, in fact) to establish processes in your business.

Process management, not to be confused with project management, takes the guesswork out of running a business. For staff, it takes the guesswork out of what to do and how. And isn't this the one thing a professional is supposed to avoid—guessing?

Process management has a serious objective, but it's not about taking the day-to-day decisions out of your hands. It's about having a set of processes that seeks continuous improvement by removing questions like "What do we do now?" or "How do we do this, again?" Some will call this a set of systems because it systematizes your operations.

Its overarching goal is getting and keeping your business so functional and streamlined that it could work as a franchise. That means, in effect, it could operate without you there to make every decision that comes along every day.

Many books outline steps to use process management as a tool for increasing revenues and streamlining efficiencies in your business. I'll provide an overview here, but this shouldn't stop you from studying the options further.

Continuous Improvement

Remember the Kaizen approach of small daily improvements that I mentioned in the last chapter? You're going to seek out those efficiencies, create a culture of continuous improvement, and use process management as one key way to do so.

Improving your operations is not always about making major changes. After a time, operations simply get wobbly in the manner that a car gets wobbly hitting all those potholes. The wheels start to come off a little bit . . . then a little bit more. Why not just tighten all the bolts at the first little shimmy, as Kaizen suggests?

Process management takes the guesswork out of the guesswork. How does it work? First let me remind you of process examples I discussed in the preceding chapters:

1. Setting goals strategically

2. Identifying and leveraging strategic competitive advantages

3. Testing and leveraging one or more revenue-generation models

4. Lining up and leveraging several strategic consumer communication approaches

Think about the components of each of those processes. How many types of goals did I ask you to set? How many ways can you continue to seek out and leverage competitive advantage? What's the step-by-step process of each revenue model, from selling your product to a buyer to collecting their money? What are the different moving parts of your communication strategy, and which staff are in charge of which ones? Those are just some strategic questions to illustrate what you'll be looking for.

That analysis of your business is the first step. Find areas that you think could benefit from some type of improvement. To do this, you have to compile as much applicable data, client commentary, and staff insights as you can find.

It's worthwhile to invite and even expect staff to participate in this improvement exercise. Believe me when I say they have ideas about improvement.

As you did with your goals, write down all your findings. Write them out so that everyone is on the same page and can correct the process and participate in the fix. When you review this data, it should include information that is both quantitative (hard data) and qualitative (information from discussions and anecdotes).

These are some additional advantages of going through these process modeling exercises and writing them down:

- Increase productivity at reduced effort and expense
- Reduce the need for heavy-handed management
- Provide staff with a sense of autonomy, direction, and ownership of their specific responsibilities
- Take the guesswork out of everyone's job

Like me, many readers operate or will open a service-based business, not a production operation in which process improvement revolves around improving the assembly line. However, we can still use the assembly line analogy when thinking about a service-based business. The assembly line starts with marketing, then moves to business development, and once the prospect signs on with your firm, they go to the operations section of the assembly line. From there, current clients roll to the customer service and client renewal stations. All these stations must run smoothly to create a business that provides you and your family with balance.

Implementing Change

After business analysis, the second step is to determine from your list of potential improvement areas what you need or want to fix first. Will you focus on the problem costing the company the most money, or the one that costs staff more work than it should? Up to you.

Before you move forward on that fix, however, you create a model of the business process you're studying. The idea is to study how a change in one part of the process affects the other parts of the process. You could use a diagram on paper or any other model that breaks the process down into its various parts.

In other words, process modeling is an attempt to create a scientific experiment that tests a dynamic system (your business). The results help you make changes and study their effects in hopes that over time you create a more efficient business.

Now that you have a model of your business and you've pinpointed areas for improvement, it's time to make one or two changes where you believe the differences can show up in your data. Here are some examples:

- Buying new software or a piece of equipment
- Training your staff on a new (or forgotten) topic
- Setting up a new schedule for a certain part of your business
- Deploying a new cold-call script for the sales department

Whatever change you put in place, you then monitor it and review the data as it arrives. The objective is to see whether and how your change affects the business and its people. Are your quarterly results better? Did your revenues improve? Did more clients renew, or did you sign on more new clients? Are employees doing less work with better results? Is the change you made sustainable and/or producing sustainable results?

After a monitoring process is over, what is the next change to make? Process management continues for as long as you believe it could be used to improve your business in any of these ways:

- Standardize the work

- Create efficiencies

- Produce more profits and/or reduce costs

- Improve the quality of the work

Ultimately the idea is to create a business so efficient, it could be turned into a franchise. You could turn over the documented process manuals to a stranger and they could make a go of it from day one by remaining faithful to your processes. This is a goal to aim for even if it's not necessarily one you'll ever want to act on. When you think franchise, you begin to appreciate the words *efficiency*, *processes*, and *procedures*. And to refresh your mind on the statistical competitive advantages of staff training, go back and review chapter 3.

Process Management and Technology

When it comes to medicine, you go to a doctor. When it comes to financing, you go to a banker or a mortgage lender. When you're in *that* kind of trouble, you find a lawyer.

When it comes to technology, it's a circus out there.

These are modern times. Before you start your business, somewhere in the early planning stage, find an information technology consultant with a wide view of the industry and an understanding of your business. Plan ways to automate your business and take advantage, as best you can, of the available technology as it applies to your operation. Find the right hardware and software, then find the connectivity (along with absolutely vital cybersecurity measures) that makes them work the way you want them to.

Then (and I know not all of you are going to love this one) train on all of it yourself. It's your business. Understand it.

When it comes to technology, it's a circus out there. Thus, even if you don't start out as a technology-dependent operation, the more success you have, the more you'll wish you had integrated basic (and more than basic) technology into your operation from day one.

Moreover, it seems necessary to say that technology changes so fast that investing in yesterday's technology can really start you off on the wrong foot. Make sure you get recent, even state-of-the-art, tech and make sure it has been tried and tested by lots of other businesses before yours.

That said, remember the goals you wrote down and hopefully tucked away in a safe place? One reason to do that was to explore who you are and what your strengths might be. Like me, you simply don't like or won't be good at a number of tasks your business needs to have done. I learned how to incorporate this tech stuff into my business strategy in a way that streamlines my business even further, uses everyone's strengths, and spares us headaches and expenses in the end. What are your strengths? What do you enjoy doing? What do you see yourself doing five and ten or more years down the line?

I mention this now as part of process management (and get into it more in chapter 9) because maybe technology is not your thing, or human resources and accounting are Greek to you. You have to know what you don't know and step aside. Step aside and bring in the experts.

That Kaizen trick says, "Ooh, Ron, please! Stop doing the bookkeeping already! You're making a mess of it." The fix is to hire an expert. It makes sense that this is about building a more efficient business, right? And—bonus! Any business job function can be out-sourced or hired in fractions of a month. You can pay the CFO for one day per month, the HR person for one recruitment campaign only, the tax pro for one day per quarter, and so on. Cost-effective.

Process management is the way to turn operations management into a science, and that's what franchises do. As I said in chapter 1, they know how to maximize efficiency. That's why nearly 12 percent of American small businesses are franchise operations. Process management is clearly documented and shared with all franchisees for success. Over 750,000 franchise businesses employ 7.5 million people and do $670 billion a year combined. They simply get operations right.[13]

Total efficiency, then, is the Holy Grail. The goal is to make your work easier, faster, more predictable, and more profitable without doing anything except working more efficiently.

---

13   Parth Parth, "Franchise Stats And Figures For Small Businesses (2024)," Vetted Biz, June 22, 2022, https://www.vettedbiz.com/franchise-and-small-business-statistics.

I hope you've understood that this is not a one-and-done exercise. Every year you study your business with the same intensity as a scientific inquiry, you get better at it. You might find some irrelevant data along the way. You may make changes that take your business the wrong way. But you can't make improvements if you don't collect data, analyze it, and make the changes you think will work. Proceed carefully, sure, but letting your business stagnate is not what good managers do.

Besides, stasis is virtually impossible. We reached a nice plateau at Amata at one point and sat on our hands for a while. Yes, we got complacent. We got lazy. It turns out you have to strive for improvements even when you think there are none to be had.

I don't improve efficiencies because it sounds good at a party. I improve the Kaizen way for these reasons:

- Every five minutes of work I save is another step toward a balanced life.

- Every dollar not spent wastefully improves the bottom line.

- Every duplicated or needlessly tedious task removed from an employee's desk makes for a happier, more productive employee.

Process management is a style of management that pushes you to find objective data and other evidence before leaping into action. But then you do take action. What you're aiming for is peak efficiency, the optimal operating status for any business that includes lower costs and a quicker path to profits.

The bottom line sounds pretty basic: Change what isn't working and focus on your company's strengths.

Chapter 7

Understand Basic Financial Management

You wouldn't jump into a swimming pool without checking the depth of the water. And you probably shouldn't jump into a business without first understanding the basics of financial management.

My primary reason for founding a business was to carve out more time for the rest of my life, but that never, ever meant I didn't pay attention to the money. You don't know anything about business money management? Learn! Learn how to follow the money.

Before delving into the specifics of financial management, let's look at a few basic principles you must understand.

1. Delegate to Professionals

Hire a professional financial management person, team, or firm to set up your accounting system, then to analyze and explain your numbers, and finally to guide your decisions from a financial perspective. No guesswork.

Hire not only an outside (objective) bookkeeping pro but also a tax professional who can do forward/strategic tax planning with you. They know procedures, deadlines, and tax law. They'll know how to qualify you for more deductions, and their specialist knowledge can identify little-known (to the average taxpayer) tax loopholes, tax-advantaged investment strategies, and so on.

Why not do these tasks yourself? If you don't know what you're doing, you need help. If you believe you know what you're doing, you need an outsider's objectivity, deep knowledge, and skill.

All that said, let's consider two different restaurants. They operate exactly alike—same menu, same staff numbers and salaries, same supply chains, same efficiencies straight down the line. There's just one exception: One business has hired an accounting firm to do the books and consults with them monthly, while the other has a brother do the books with no outside experts around at all.

The brother has no formal training and will miss most allowed deductions. The brother will not know the current year's changes in the tax code. The brother might not know the filing deadlines or rules (especially for payroll).

Bring in professionals to identify financial efficiencies beyond production or services. Not only are financial efficiencies safer but they may make the difference between a one-week vacation once a year or four weeks spent with your family twice a year.

Every year I learn something new from my accountants and tax advisors, and so should you. A relationship-oriented financial advisor is exactly what you need.

2. Set up Checks and Balances

It's imperative that someone who does *not* have any power over company finances reviews the checkbook and the account balances regularly.

Why? It happens all too often: embezzlement, fraud, theft, misappropriation, robbery, pilfering. Partners steal from partners, or people you believe are nothing more than bespectacled church ladies can't help themselves and reach into the cookie jar. Ask any independent accountant or CPA how prevalent this cheating and theft really are. They see it every month. They'll tell you how many owners don't suspect a thing till tax time—or later. Beyond this, checks and balances guard against your own personal foibles. We all have spending impulses to guard against; some just do it more strictly than others.

Don't underestimate the potential of personal crowdfunding.

Put glibly, the more you don't think you need checks and balances, the more you need them.

3. Diversify Your Funding Options

You should know two things about starting a business:

1. You'll have to bankroll at least three months and more likely up to six months of cash flow by yourself, or you'll need to borrow to

get started and/or get through some of the business's low-cash periods.

2. There are many funding sources, but only two *types* of money: Outside money you have to pay to use, such as a loan with interest, and personal money you forfeit interest to use, such as your own money, a grant (no interest and no paying back), or help from a friend or a relative (presumably no interest).

Right up there with the free money called grants, many local governments offer tax breaks for setting up shop in their jurisdiction.

Needless to say, borrowed money is the funding of last resort, but it ends up being an unfortunate necessity for many businesspeople starting things up. Starting out on a shoestring budget is challenging, but you'll look back on the experience with pride.

Don't underestimate the potential of personal crowd-funding, a method this fellow I'm going to tell you about used. As the story goes, a shipping magnate named George Steinbrenner purchased the New York Yankees in 1973 for $10 million. Although the rest of the numbers are conjecture here, the interesting part of the story is that he paid only a pittance of his own money—the storyteller said $5,000—while he found friends to put up the rest.

He recruited these people by signing contracts that said he would buy them out when he could. The profits the New York Yankees made then went into Steinbrenner's bank account, and he used that money to pay back his friends. In the end, he simply let the Yankees pay off his friends, and he owned the entire team.

With that in mind, if you have a winning formula (the Yankees were already making a profit), you might interest your friends and family in a financial stake. Still, you'll also want to leave no stone unturned in your search for alternate funding sources. Let me remind you that funding is not only money/cash. It's sometimes available in other forms:

- Money you choose not to spend (just pass on making that purchase for now)
- Wholesale (bulk purchase) discounts
- Barters with other businesses (trading products or services instead of purchasing them)

When push comes to shove, sure, you may have to borrow. Negotiate for the best terms you can. Shop around among local banks, and remember credit unions too. Shorter loans are almost always advantageous compared to long-term loans, just as paying principal ahead of time can significantly lower interest costs.

4. Don't Pay Interest; Earn It

The minute you start a business—even before you open your doors, actually—you must train yourself to know, understand, believe, appreciate, and embrace the concept that money is alive.

Of course, it isn't alive, but the metaphor is too critical to dispute. Money has life. Each dollar bill has life.

There's a scene in the movie *Sideways* in which Virginia Madsen's character explains why she loves wine. She says when she drinks wine she thinks about the day the grapes were harvested and the people involved in its production. She adores the idea that a wine's flavor changes day to day, so if you opened it sooner rather than later it would taste different, "because a bottle of wine is actually alive," she says.

That's the kind of aliveness I'm talking about. Money not only grows and shrinks day to day based on where you place it, but the economic environment changes value and purchasing power constantly. Inflation, the value of the dollar on the open market, the level of volatility in the stock market, the prices of commodities—all these and more can nibble at or nourish your private bank account.

More fundamental and much closer to home is the simple idea that paying interest on a loan will, without fail, make you work harder, while earning interest on your investments will allow you to work less.

As much as possible, then, avoid debt. Put a portion of your profits aside in conservative investments that pay you interest or dividends. Companies can do that. Yours should, too.

5. Practice Financial Discipline

As a matter of financial discipline (and get help to crunch the numbers if needed), make sure your profits and not your savings or your cash flow are paying for the loans you take out.

Discipline also requires you to understand the difference between principal and interest—especially that compound interest can work against you if it's adding up and you're the one paying it, or it can work for you if you're the one collecting it.

Steinbrenner might have sounded like a rich tightwad unwilling to take a risk by himself, but the other way to look at it is that he was very, very disciplined with his money and understood how money works. He had financial discipline.

You either pay to use money or you don't. If your business is going to survive the hard times, you have to rely on cash flow instead of running to the bank every time it hits a pothole. Cash flow will bail you out without forcing you to pay interest on the money you spend.

Financial discipline is about spending when you have to and paying the lowest prices you can, saving as much as possible, making safe investments, reducing taxes to a minimum, and paying your bills and taxes on time so you avoid late fees. This wisdom is sometimes undermined by that little voice in your head that confuses luxury and necessity.

We always hear, "Never put your own money at risk." On paper, that sounds great. In practice, it isn't always easy to find outside funding—lenders want you to have some skin in the game by putting up a percentage of the money yourself. Still, it's sound thinking: Keep your own money out of the loop whenever you can.

Build your team of advisors to double-check your numbers and spending plans. Whether you're an impulsive spender or a penny pincher, put in some checks and balances so that no one employee has an all-access pass to your money. Make sure you assemble a conservative group when it comes to financial matters, meaning they help you *conserve* as much money as possible.

6. Reward Your Team

If you like spending, reward your staff and your principal advisors. That's the kind of spending that pays you back.

The need to reward your team well, in so many words, should be as clear and obvious to employers as the need to feed your children. But the circumstances of two different companies are never exactly the same, so it's up to entrepreneurs to set the bar on compensation. How do you make that decision?

This is where good, solid human resource professionals come into play, and it's one of the reasons I advocate loud and clear for outsourcing your key positions.

It's 2024. You can't guess or throw a dart at a wall to determine what to pay your people. The job and pay markets are all over the map for some reasons you know and some you never will. As you can imagine, those who perform due diligence on their compensation are your employees. They know better than you what your competitors are paying and how they rank among their peers in your company.

Yes, there are strategies to set compensation based on an employee's direct value to the company. Pay them a little more than average? Pay them the highest wage in your field? Pay them average, but add in generous perks? Each of these options is available. Perks can be an economic way to reward employees, but nothing eclipses take-home pay. Everyone should have some scalable value to the company. Survey your competition. What are they paying?

Then there's something called reality. Start-up companies and those going through a sustained rough patch have fewer options and less cash available. That doesn't mean you can't reward your crew. Face reality. Then tell your workers you're willing to support them fully (Amata found a way to do that, as I mentioned earlier, when an employee lost his eyesight and finally came back to work; we changed our benefits package for everyone to serve him better).

Provide the most solid training you can imagine and then add to that. Provide generous letters of recommendation. In a year or so, they may jump ship. That should be the goal. You don't want to hold people down out of desperation. Take on someone else who is new, train them, support them, and send them on their way. Think it through. Have you done everything you can for them? Everything? Really? Then we're on the same page.

7. Measure Your Results

Measurement of results is another form of checks and balances. In this case, as promoted extensively by John Doerr, author of *Measure What Matters,* the idea begins with acknowledging that inefficiencies that often slip by are simply a matter of waste. You should also acknowledge that every decision can go awry through unexpected factors or simply because not every decision is a slam dunk or a grand slam.

Measuring results, of course, is a fundamental aspect of process management, which would have you track every process in your company that impacts the bottom line. Measure to get back on track, stay the course, reach your goals, and correct inefficiencies.

Chapter 8

Develop a Sales Cycle

Since I'm a sales guy, you might be bracing yourself for a long, long chapter here. No. That's because the basic steps of a sales cycle have been laid out in numerous sales books and discussed in countless seminars and conferences. Read. Go to training. Learn. You can do that, and you must because there's (almost) nothing more important to your business than making sales.

Many instructors break down the steps differently or give the steps names of their own. Don't be fooled. It all boils down to ABC:

A. Find a customer.

B. Make a deal at a price point allowing you a profit.

C. Nurture your relationship with that customer to make more sales.

The sales cycle should include prospect generation, discovery, proposal, implementation, and post-sale activity. But this is a slightly jargon-heavy way of saying find customers, make the pitch and the close, then follow up with excellent service—in other words, ABC.

Study your technique. Over time, make the necessary tweaks based on the results your own in-house examination reveals.

Let's look at sales from a process management perspective. Prospect generation starts, of course, with marketing, and marketing can be broken down into various activities as well. Do you market your services online or in other media? Do you do marketing through events, like conferences, expositions, or awards presentations? Try to keep track of all those activities, then send periodic surveys to clients to track which of those options are most effective.

Discovery is another word for listening, but it implies very active listening. Discovery is like mining for copper, but using your ears, eyes, and focus to pick up clues from your clients about what they really want. Why? So you can give it to them, of course.

A proposal, meanwhile, is an outline of a contract that spells out goals, specific challenges, and solutions your company will provide. For any substantial deal, this is done in writing, but verbal agreements prior to contract signing occur all the time.

Once you initiate this process, however, it becomes not a chore but a comfort. It's comforting to know you have a systematic approach that can be studied and made to work efficiently and productively. With process management, you won't be guessing about how a deal can be made. Make it a step-by-step process so you can work toward an efficient method of doing business. Winging it is not an option. Get that system in place. This is no time for guesswork.

How to Grow Sales Without Selling

My pet distinction here revolves around the simple concept of service. Let me repeat myself: Companies with high levels of service do better at retaining customers and making profits than those that don't.

In this regard, the fundamental mistake I see is that companies take their customers for granted. It's very hard and expensive to find a customer and close a deal in the first place. But then many companies think their work is done. They let established customers slip through their fingers. They don't remember to nurture those relationships or make them grow.

Don't do that. Go back to chapter 5 on communicating with those who are making your business a success.

A customer signing a deal with you is giving you their trust. They've made a fundamental decision that you are on their team, that you are the supplier or the service that is right for them. Their expectations are at an all-time high; they've signed a deal or forked over some money in a gesture of goodwill. If after that you let the customer slip through your fingers, then you've given up the opportunity to make much, much easier sales.

The first sale is the hardest. After that, current customers are low-hanging fruit ripe for a harvest of additional sales. They already like your product or your services. You want to keep that smile on their face as long as possible.

Let's say you sell a customer a big-ticket item like a swimming pool, expecting there will be no other sales forthcoming. What a mistake! Cleaning products, cleaning services, fences, pool toys, various apparatus, pumps and filters, leak detection services, lounge chairs, deck umbrellas—not to mention maintenance contracts—can be sold to that customer. Those complimentary products can be more profitable over time than even the most expensive pool might have been.

The smartphone industry demonstrates this very nicely. One after the other, phone carriers have subsidized the prices of expensive phones, understanding that the service contracts will more than make up the difference.

Home office and commercial printer manufacturers do this as well. The price of the printer itself is often remarkably low. But the manufacturers would rather get the printer to you cheap and make continuous earnings on ink cartridges and periodic maintenance than sell you a very expensive printer and never see you again.

In effect, the sales process never ends and should continue to flourish with follow-up products and services until the market shifts dramatically or the zebra changes its stripes.

At Amata, like at most companies, we work extremely hard at finding and securing customers through marketing and various sales activities. We develop office space for lawyers, and after we earn their trust and they sign up to use our space or services, our sales work is just beginning.

Let me more or less repeat myself on this, because it's so important: A recent figure that makes sense to me is that customer-centric businesses are 60 percent more profitable than other companies.[14] And remember, 86 percent of customers are willing to pay more for a better experience with a company.[15]

> **Understand what your sales cycle is going to be and have realistic expectations.**

An experience is not sales, you say? Stop. Please. Excellent service, it turns out, is the required marketing step to make additional sales. This includes the very old-fashioned

---

14   Dorothea Schmidt, Dominik Moulliet, Alexander Majonek, and Florian Grimm, *Wealth Management Digitalization Changes Client Advisory More Than Ever Before* (Deloitte, 2017).

15   Farrell, "PwC: Consumers Will Pay More for Better Experience."

skills of following through on promises and listening carefully.

Again, Frank and I had a very basic understanding of our business on day one, and our business grew (and grew and grew) primarily through the ageless tradition of listening to people. In other words, our sales grew by creating customer-centric experiences. Great customer service is really the name of the game.

Waiting Through the Sales Cycle

You need to understand what your sales cycle is going to be and have realistic expectations. When you see how long it takes from first contact to first payment by the typical consumer, you can then sit with your financial advisor and determine how much cash flow you need to cover bills till sales revenue starts coming in. It's very important both in the early days and throughout your business's existence.

If I'm talking to a new law firm about taking office space, that sales cycle could be anywhere from five to eight months. I know that now. I can't expect to see that revenue immediately. That's the cycle for making a sale in my business. Your business will be different, of course. That's why having professionals crunch your numbers to determine this cycle is so vital.

There's never been a case when I start talking to a prospect and the next day they sign. It doesn't happen, no matter how good a salesperson I am. There's no relationship yet, no rapport or trust. The majority of my clients become clients after I spend time nurturing that relationship, building their trust, being transparent when I answer their questions, being honest, and giving them references as requested. And so on.

If you're starting a new business, you need to understand what that sales cycle is. Ask around. If your CPA or tax person has a number of clients (no, they won't reveal secrets) that are similar to your business, they may have a clearer idea of your sales cycle than you do in the beginning. It doesn't hurt to ask.

Once the sale has closed, your post-sale activity should follow the guidelines I gave in chapter 5 on communication strategies. For many businesses, including mine, that's where the most business revenue comes from—ongoing contact with existing clients and customers. Make communication part of the sales cycle and you'll do just fine.

Chapter 9

Hire or Outsource?

Let me take you back to my early words on life balance. Everywhere in life, there's a role we play: son, daughter, parent, spouse, teacher, minister, cowboy, soldier, cook, artist, athlete, and . . . entrepreneur.

Granted, entrepreneur is an odd role to play. There isn't a well-established guidebook for entrepreneurs even though there are many of us. It isn't the same as being CEO of a huge corporation. It's not like being a solopreneur or freelancer, either.

The picture of the typical American entrepreneur is hard to paint. But let's try a composite sketch and see how far we can go:

- An entrepreneur has defined goals and knows where they will be in five years.

- An entrepreneur knows a lot about money, how to work with banks or accountants, or how to raise a bit of capital when opportunities arise.

- An entrepreneur is hungry to keep up with business and industry trends, dresses sharp, has an impressive vocabulary, and drives a new car.

- An entrepreneur is also diplomatic, knowing the next opportunity might come from a surprising place.

- An entrepreneur sees business as serious stuff.

- An entrepreneur is a hard worker. There's no way around that if you have serious dreams and financial goals.

- An entrepreneur has a strong ego. This is a positive but also an Achilles heel. Too much ego can topple even the strongest structures.

Carly Fiorina was the first woman to lead a major technology company when she became the CEO of Hewlett-Packard (HP) in 1999; she held the position till 2005. After some other endeavors, she founded a small business and reportedly said, "It was easier as CEO of a large corporation filled with specialist talent. I have to be a Jill-of-All-Trades in this small operation!"

True words. It's an exhausting state to be in—unless you remember your need for life balance and your ability to outsource or hire specialist talent.

Avoiding Overwork and Managing Ego

Watch for the signs. Since this is a book about keeping your balance, it seems appropriate to note the warning signs of overwork: headaches at night; one too many drinks more often than you like; restlessness/never feeling rested; kids leaving the room when you enter. You get the idea.

But my purpose here is to give you the proactive approach, to tell you how I learned to avoid some of the pitfalls of overwork and an over-boiling ego. It comes down to three things to do regularly.

1. Ask and Assess

Where am I at with balance in my life? How many hours did I work this week—and why? What leisure with loved ones and alone did I enjoy this week—or why did I miss it?

2. Stay Goal-Focused

If you want to keep your balance, you must anticipate problems and maintain a focus on your personal goals. You need goals that balance out work, such as health goals, community goals, family goals, and spiritual goals. Keep them intact and unflinching. Keep your eye on the prize: a healthy, balanced, rewarding life. Don't let your work goals compromise your life goals. Unless you were born in a bottle, that can't possibly lead to happiness.

3. Remember Your Goals
In the first chapters of this book, I asked you to write down your lifetime goals and take them out once every six months. Take them out now. Check to make sure they're intact.

What does all that lead-in have to do with a chapter on hiring versus outsourcing? I'm going to tell you now.

Hiring and Managing Your People

They say that hiring is the first luxury of business. When you start out doing everything, what could be more luxurious than paying someone do to part of your job? Your business has grown enough to cover a regular monthly payroll. Celebrate! Then think hard about who you should hire to do what in the business.

Before you hire, identify necessary work that you enjoy doing and work that gives you a headache. Hiring for the work in the second category, if you manage it well, will keep you sane and young and save you a lot of money in aspirin.

The mistake many entrepreneurs make is micro-managing, and that's about trust. Micromanaging your employees generally means you've failed to unburden yourself of the chore you didn't enjoy. You can call this double jeopardy: You still do two jobs, and now you have to pay a new employee on top of that. If you can't let go and trust those who work for you, running a growing business is going to be difficult.

Great People Make Mistakes

The antidote to micromanaging can be summed up as letting your employees make mistakes—and correct them on their own as much as possible. Don't beat them up for making mistakes; instead, help them understand where they went wrong and learn from it.

Give them freedom to err. It's healthier for you and a relief (and motivation) for your employees. You need to enjoy life. They need to learn their jobs, commit to the company, and grow accordingly. For years, I've told my people no one gets in trouble for making a mistake. The only time you'll hear me get upset is if you didn't make a decision and it cost us something. I'd rather have a mistake than indecision. If it's the wrong decision, we'll learn from that together. Learning something makes it a good day, whereas indecision serves no purpose.

You have to ask yourself what kind of relationship you want with your staff.

I know that making mistakes bonds people together. I'm convinced this is how you get employees to stay with you fifteen or twenty years or more. They feel safe (and trusted) working in an environment in which mistakes aren't considered lethal. How can you relax without that in place? This leads employees to own their mistakes by tying the quality of their work to emotions that are part of their lives.

You also have to ask yourself what kind of relationship you want with your staff. No one wants a job where they are constantly looking over their shoulder; intimidation or anger is not the way you want to be remembered.

All that said, you aren't looking for the opposite side of the spectrum, either. You want independent employees, not ones who constantly seek you out for advice and direction. I've had administrators on my staff who needed me in the loop on everything they did. I eventually just stopped answering questions from those who wouldn't stop coming to me at every turn.

Yes, stop answering questions. This is not the type of advice I expect to see in most business management textbooks. It's about hiring the people with the right skills, experience, and knowledge to do the job and to own their decisions, right or wrong. Who knew employees would actually feel more attached to their jobs if you allowed them to savor the growth they are provided? Work is more meaningful when you own it completely. If you don't allow employees to own their jobs, they resent the absolutes you thrust on them.

If your ego enjoys having someone asking you questions, you've fallen into an ego trap, and no trap is good. Remind yourself why you hired them; trust their experience and judgment. Let them own their decisions so they grow in the job, and you have the opportunity for a balanced life.

Over time, I realized some other ancillary benefits of allowing employees to make mistakes and learn from them: much better buy-in to the company's mission, greater loyalty, and a greater sense of pride in their work.

When They Say Goodbye
Only a boss fully understands the time and expense it takes to train a new employee. With today's very

uniquely shaped labor force, all we hear about is how fickle the American worker is. Remote work is a blessing and a curse.

I believe the fear of replacing workers who have empowered themselves or been trained well (and then move on) is overblown. We can't fault our workers for knowing their value in the marketplace and pursuing their career goals.

Let me remind you of process management, in which recruitment is very much a part of the overall processes you map out. One of the prime benefits of running an efficient operation is the gain you make in training new employees. If everything is honed to its simplest methodology and the business is sure of its goals and techniques, you should be able to hire and train (replicate, if you will) a departed employee without losing a minute's sleep.

Outsourcing

To me, it's hard to imagine a businessperson who loves every aspect of running a business or is skilled at all the jobs that come with running a smooth operation. If your company is growing, it's because one daring entrepreneur has done a great job at getting the company going.

Now that daring person needs help: You find that more and more often, you're banging your head against the wall, doing all the jobs that need to get done. Growth of the business allowed you to hire, but you've said, "I can't afford real managers or highly skilled specialist staff just yet. I'll still do all that myself." When your company has fewer than ten employees, you can probably get along doing it all, sure. Then suddenly you need these professionals.

In a panic, you realize recruiting and hiring new personnel has become half your job—and not the half you enjoy very much. Enter the need for an HR manager.

In a panic, you hear software program XYZ has crashed, and you're the only one who knows what to do. Enter the need for an IT team.

Three weeks have gone by, and with horror you realize your bookkeeping is behind. Enter the need for an accountant (perhaps led by a controller).

And of course, here's the real panic: This is beginning to look expensive because now some of the functions your business needs are *not* revenue-generating.

The breaking point comes sooner than you expect.

Wouldn't it be nice if you could find an eight-hour-per-week HR specialist? Is that even possible? Yes, it actually is. Wouldn't it be nice to have a CFO on tap, maybe just a full day twice a month? Yes, that's possible, too.

I fell into this trap myself. HR gobbled up my time without adding directly to my sense of achievement. I wasn't keeping up, and I needed help.

And this is where the beauty of outsourcing comes into play. You no longer have to pay a highly experienced, highly effective expert full-time when you need one only a few hours a month. Outsourcing is the elegant option simply because I want and receive expert help, but I don't have to pay the annual salary (plus benefits, office, and equipment) of a full-time employee with that expertise. It could be the difference between paying $90,000 gross annual salary plus benefits and equipment and paying just $18,000 in billable (productively worked) hours each year. For the business owner following the money, it's an obvious choice.

Since their specialty is all they do, they stay up-to-date and enjoy their work. Furthermore, the arrangement is labor friendly. If you hire a specialist to work for you and cutbacks are needed, you don't have to lay anyone off. You just cut back on the services. Outsourcing provides a labor market cushion and a great transition from no one at all in the position to a full-time employee as your companies business requires it and you can justify the expense.

Human resources was my first outsourced professional. It was quickly clear that this was more efficient than doing things myself or hiring someone full-time when it was far too early in the business's development. When Amata grew to about fifty employees, I still outsourced my HR because I'm not an expert in this field and I don't want to be. It turns out it's a lot cheaper to have an expert working for another firm do my HR work than it is for me to hire my own personnel, because I can't make use of scale the way a specialty firm does.

Before I started Amata, I ran an outsourcing company myself, covering 250 law firms that outsourced all their central staff employees. These were the staff who answered their phones, managed records, sorted mail, made copies, and handled data entry and similar tasks.

Outsourcing gives you the famous 100 percent utilization that you can never achieve in your own shop. Business is about efficiency because efficiency means profit. If you want a balanced life, every small adjustment that adds to company efficiency will get you closer to the lifestyle you want.

Having said all that, here's my short message: You can outsource a part-time (aka fractional) leadership team. This includes HR management and every other executive, managerial, or key employee or specialist your business needs. Virtually any job you need to hire for can be hired on a part-time, outsourced basis.

The options for outsourcing I've listed here may have marginal interest to you as you're starting out, but starting out is the perfect time to consider these ser- vices—and to interview candidates who can fulfill your future needs. For instance, why stumble around trying to set up, figure out, and then do something you hate or just aren't good at? Finding an outsourced expert right at the start can save you needless frustrations (not to mention time to fix what you did wrong later, and money to perform that fix).

Let's look at some of the most important roles you should consider outsourcing.

Accountant

So many people don't see this coming, I have to repeat what I've already said about it: Handling your company's money always requires a system of checks and balances. Always.

This refers all but exclusively to the necessity of separating those who balance the books from those who write the checks. If it's the same person, the temptations clearly get the better of many people who start off as honest, diligent, loyal, and completely trustworthy. Separating the money counters from those with rights to the company's checks and credit cards is a fundamental step in protecting your company from an embarrassing form of theft—the kind that occurs because you weren't paying attention.

In addition, hiring an accountant or a team of accountants has opened up significant personal gain for me that also benefits my business. This should be true of all outsourcing services anyway. The practice I'm referring to is the simple act of meeting periodically with your outsourced personnel.

I recommend interviewing several accountants to identify the ones who are also willing to meet with and teach you. This goes for many of life's opportunities: You should nurture your curiosity and see what growth working with these professionals can provide.

Lawyer

Most lawyers practice in specialized areas. You want a business or corporate lawyer at the beginning. You'll need to select the type of formation to incorporate your business, and you'll likely have contracts to draft or receive contracts to review before you sign. Don't handle contracts yourself—consult a professional not just for their knowledge but for their objectivity. When you're fighting for your own self-interests, you can lose sight of the long-term objectives and get tangled up in unnecessary skirmishes.

Business Coach/Consultant

This is usually a profession that bills you on a monthly retainer, but ask.

If your goal is to maintain your life balance, there can be no greater asset than a seasoned business coach or consultant. They, too, specialize somewhat. Some are family business consultants, while others are start-up consultants, and so on. You probably want a general business consultant who understands strategic planning for growth. There are several reasons for this.

First, not every entrepreneur studied business in school. Some simply started from scratch or found themselves holding the reins to a business through promotion or random circumstance. A business coach can take you from flying by the seat of your pants to operating as a seasoned business manager over time.

Another reason is that even MBA graduates have to face the fact that business in the real world is often surprisingly different from the academic models they studied. A business coach can help you adjust and learn to cope with real-world challenges in real time.

Everybody also needs help maintaining an objective perspective on life, especially the parts of life that have emotional aspects to them. In this regard, owning a business may sound like an enterprise in which emotional baggage plays no part, but that is one hundred percent myth and zero percent reality. Of course, we put in our heart and soul and place handsome ego-laden bets on every decision we make, including those having to do with the ice-cold activity we call running a business.

Let's not kid ourselves. Business is an activity in which our sense of perspective is not always a given (either lack of knowledge or ego gets in the way). A business coach is another professional who remains objective for you.

A business coach can also help you define personal as well as business goals that may be hard for you to figure out—especially if you tell them your overall strategy is achieving life balance by creating a business that serves you and not the contrary. They can help devise and implement strategies to achieve that.

Financial Consultant

What do you know about annuities? What do you know about the insurance business? Do you know how and when your stock market investments are taxed? Do you know the differences between IRA accounts? What do you know about retirement planning or the taxes you might owe in twenty-five years? What do you know about gifts and inheritance? The future effects of inflation?

If your answer to any of those questions is "Um" or "Well . . ." or "I'll get back to you on that," then you could certainly benefit from the services of a financial advisor, a certified management accountant (CMA), or a chartered financial consultant (ChFC).

Related to this function, consult a strategic tax professional. You might find you no longer owe $14,500 in taxes (as you self-calculated) but zero (the expert finding!). You just don't know what you don't know. Consult professionals.

Part III

Destination Checklist: An Exit Strategy for a Balanced Life

Chapter 10

Make Decisions with Your Exit Strategy in Mind

An exit strategy is not just about retirement, but truly about how to exit the business—sell it, close it, turn it over to offspring—when you decide that you've had enough fun and it's time to move on to new things. It could be a plan for five years from now or for when you turn seventy-five years of age. It's up to you, but *plan* is the operative word here.

I was at a law firm the other day, talking to the managing partner. It's a midsized law firm with about a hundred attorneys. The partner told me about another attorney whose son was moving to Norway or one of those countries that makes it easy for an expat to get dual citizenship. The son didn't tell Dad he was moving until Dad came to visit and saw Son was already packing to leave a week later with his wife.

Son said, "I got enough money to retire on. So this is it."

Dad said, "No, no, no, you don't. Why didn't you talk to me about this?"

Son responded, "I didn't talk to you because you would try to talk me out of it."

Son was in his late twenties or early thirties. So, yeah, he probably hadn't saved nearly enough. And, yeah, Dad was in fact trying to make him see reason.

Dad came to the partner telling me this. The partner said to him, "You and I know he doesn't have enough money to retire. But let your son go. He'll discover it when he needs a major medical procedure or something happens to one of his investments that he didn't foresee. He'll be back in the States when he realizes he has to work."

That story got me thinking. We're starting our business for a specific reason, but nothing's permanent. At some point you'll want to leave it, or it will leave you.

How do you know when it's time to exit, or even how to engineer an exit? When it's time to sell the business, you wonder how much you can get for it and whether you built it up enough. You wonder whether you could be an employee again if you're that young and already thinking about exiting your business. You wonder (as we all hope Son did) whether you could actually stop working and still provide for yourself and the family. You wonder whether you could find something else to occupy your mind and time without the structure and activity work gives you, and that's probably the bigger question.

These are legitimate questions. Maybe the answers prove you're not ready to exit. Money is just one reason to do so.

Many times, people don't make more money by starting their business. They end up working more hours. They might go from making seventy-five dollars an hour working for someone else to making fifteen an hour in their own business. When they calculate how many hours they have to work for themselves, they can end up working for less than minimum wage. You might exit a business like that because you have no life balance and the purpose of the business (provide a living) has failed you.

I know attorneys who don't see a difference between loving one thing (their work) and not knowing something else they might do with their life. Let me say this: If you've been doing it for so long you don't know what else to do, that might be a reason to exit.

Also ask yourself, "Am I exiting the business because I hate it as much as the job I had before?" If you're running from it and don't know what you're running toward, you have to rethink your goals. You didn't keep the end goal in mind, maybe, or you didn't think through the six dimensions of your personal goals.

Here's a thought that is not at all new in this millennium: You might be forced to exit due to changing technologies. If you're in a tech business or you offer very tech-driven services, you need a strategy to move on or adapt, or you'll get innovated out of business at some point.

We often have some misconceptions when we start a business:

1. I'll be doing this for the rest of my life.

2. I'll sell it and move on when the business is worth $10 million.

3. I'll do this till I'm fifty. That's it.

4. I'll do this till my personal net worth is $5 million.

5. I'll do this until one of my kids wants to take it over.

I was the first case. I thought, "Boy, this is fun. I can't see myself doing anything else." Whatever little idea you have about how long you'll be in that business, you can't ignore the reality that you have to plan for what comes next. You need a plan that tells you when and how to exit. Your strategy will be related to your end goal, the one we talked about way back at the start of the book.

Behind every exit strategy, whatever it may be, is something called wealth. As we've discovered by now, the theme of this book is the surprising way in which efficiencies can increase your wealth. This type of thinking helps when transitions come along, retirement included. Hopefully you and your financial advisor figured this out a long time ago. But in the meantime, it helps to understand where your transitioning business fits into the greater scheme of things. So one of the fundamental things you need to ask is whether your business will still be valuable when you're no longer running it.

Separate Yourself from Your Business

If you take a healthy, balanced approach and push that exit strategy idea to its furthest point, you get to the question of what your business is worth without you. What's it worth to someone else? Step away from the day-to-day chores and stresses of work to find the answers to two more questions.

1. Does your trusty little business hum right along in your absence, and how well? This is, as you now know, a question about the completeness and efficiency of your process management.

2. How well do *you* function sitting on a beach or biking through the woods while your business is plugging along with other people calling the shots? This is, as you also now know, about the goals you set (or don't set) for your personal life.

It's no secret that some very dedicated worker bees have a difficult time figuring out what to do in their retirement years. They pick up a camera and start taking pictures, then figure out a month later that it isn't working out. They travel for a bit, and this novelty, too, runs out of steam. They can't find traction gardening in the backyard, building birdhouses, or volunteering at the local library reference desk after the rough-and-tumble highs and lows of running a business. They enjoyed their time wrestling gators in the business world. Parking the car at a scenic pull-off on a lonely stretch of road and painting watercolor landscapes just doesn't do it for them.

This brings us full circle, of course, right back to the goals you should have written down and updated at least once a year back before you even started your business. We need goals, as you should have considered in chapter 2, in six dimensions or more of your life—physical, mental, emotional, spiritual, social/leisure, vocational/educational—and you should be making progress in all of them. Retirement is a great time to activate at least the last three of these.

Those goals are sometimes what holds us together. If you were sincere about reading every day to keep your mind occupied and your knowledge base growing, then you've likely arrived at the realization that great things come in small increments. It's that Kaizen thing again. You don't suddenly read Charles Dickens's entire catalog overnight. You journey along day by day, making steady, bite-sized progress.

You should also be concerned about discovery along the way because there are those who have difficulty finding that cheerful little hobby that perfectly rounds out their lifelong ambitions. Some find playing a musical instrument provides more frustration than rewards, while others realize the dream of a lifetime in learning to play. The time to nurture those interests is right now. It's unlikely that you'll wake up some morning in your sixties and suddenly see the light regarding a fulfilling hobby. These interests don't pop up out of nowhere.

Sometimes we pick up a hobby and find it just isn't challenging enough. The problem isn't the hobby itself, but the intrinsic value of defining a difficult goal can help. Don't just take pictures; take extraordinary pictures. Don't just paint landscapes; set the bar higher. Paint extraordinary landscapes.

If you have to train yourself to enjoy life, start small.

Travel, of course, is one way to move forward without regrets. Of all the time I've spent in this life, some of the most rewarding has been behind the steering wheel of an RV, chugging along a four-hour route around this fascinating country of ours with my family.

Not every day is the Fourth of July or Christmas or Thanksgiving. But we can bring our personal goals with us wherever we go. A family trip doesn't derail my goals of staying in shape and reading something interesting each night before I go to sleep. It doesn't cancel out my goals of remaining happily married or attentive to my children. Why would it do that? For me, it never has. It's about the journey, remember?

Keeping your balance while running your business as well as while living your outside-of-business life requires a bit of personal sacrifice, mostly the willingness to give up control. Walking away from your business shouldn't mean white-knuckling it through the day, expecting some dreaded phone call about how your business collapsed without your magic touch on every decision, large and small.

If you have to train yourself to enjoy life, start small. One fellow I talked to had one little goal per day in the early days of his retirement—one new thing he'd try or go back to, with no pressure to spend more than a couple of hours at it that day. That worked not only to give him the structure he missed for a few hours of each day but also to slowly develop new interests.

Take a Sabbatical

Did you know a sabbatical is a break from one's regular job lasting from one month to two years? Don't break out in a sweat. You can define what it means for you, in your specific circumstance, all by yourself.

Salaried people envy us because it seems to be a given in their minds that entrepreneurs can take a sabbatical, a vacation, or time away almost at will. Many entrepreneurs are free-spirited types with busy minds and an intrinsic curiosity about the world. They're ambitious and know how to get things done. Why wouldn't they be eager, willing, and able to take time off from work for interesting, rewarding adventures of their own choosing? But other business owners find themselves glued to their Puritan work ethics, feeling secure and safe only when confronted with the challenges of running their businesses. They live in a myopic, nine-to-five (or nine-to-nine) cocoon. And while this might feel comfortable for a time, in order to grow, you have to seek out fresh ideas. You have to get out of the office once in a while.

Granted, taking a month off out of the blue is a scary proposition. Start with just one day off if that's what it takes. I know a married couple running their own consultancy who finally challenged their "We can walk away" boast. They went MIA every Friday. No office, no email, and no phone. Staff were politely asked to "deal with it," whatever "it" was. It was scary the first few weeks, but now it's their schedule every week, and they never work on the weekend. Work up to it.

Along the way, you're testing your priorities. The idea isn't to take an hour off and waste the hour but to explore the other half of your life, the half that includes family, recreation, and personal development. All those lifelong goals you wrote down before you became an entrepreneur—this is the time to make those dreams come true.

How much time will you dedicate to the business? A harsher question is this: How many hours a week are you just doing busy work, pretending to work when there's none to do? Aha—busted! Like hiring a couple of consultants, once your business is up and running, your efficient process management should be allowing you to enjoy days like that—so go out. Get lost. Leave the office. Turn off your phone.

My real point is that you should already be asking yourself how many hours you wish to spend at work and what type of schedule you want to keep. Do this right from the start, and not only will staff be used to it, so will you. A balanced life requires some time to yourself every week and, honestly, every day. Most exercise regimes call for daily effort; it is said that playing tennis every day is exercise, while playing tennis only on weekends is what we call stress.

Change Your Lifestyle

Look through your list of goals. In all likelihood, some will require daily effort (physical exercise or meditation time), while others will be best realized by taking a week or a month off from work. And some, such as staying connected with your children and spouse, require a little bit of both. Depending on their ages, you'll need daily interactions with your children to stay in the loop and then, as they age, this might dwindle just a bit. But sometimes your loved ones require longer interactions—a week or two, maybe a month or more.

At some point achieving your lifelong goals will boil down to doing something that can be very difficult: making serious lifestyle changes. Without going into deep psychology here, humans are creatures of habit and even prone to destructive addictions. It's part of our nature. Cigarettes, alcohol, overeating, overworking, gaming or sex addiction, computers, drugs, golf, jogging, whole-body tattoos, even compulsive

weightlifting/working out—the list of potential addictions is well known. Certainly, some of those vices start
out as benign, even healthy. But before you know it,
they can end up pursuing you in the form of addictions
you didn't even know existed.

So, it's easy to say that lifestyle changes are critical but
difficult to know exactly how to make them happen.
Once again, there are simply times when you need to
embrace your goals fully to live the healthy balance
that affords you personal success and experiences
that satisfy your soul.

The process of setting and achieving goals can be
an acquired taste. Start small; don't overreach.
Appreciate the journey it takes to understand, enjoy,
and appreciate minor victories. Big achievements are
really the culmination of thousands of small steps
fueled by persistence, vision, and dedication—Kaizen
again. Humanity didn't reach the moon without string-
ing together a few million small advances first. We just
don't often stop to think about it that way.

Expand Your Growth Mindset

Businesses don't have to grow, but they tend to find
their point of maximum return. If there's room to grow
and the opportunity presents itself, it's human nature,
as much as anything else, that propels us forward.

And financial gain is not the only factor that creates the need for growth.

To see my point, it helps to expand your idea of what growth might be. Our society is clearly dedicated to the notion that growth means more products or services sold, more profits made, more jobs created, more net wealth, and more parking spots needed. The key word is *more*.

Entrepreneurs do enjoy serving a need and fulfilling a purpose. They enjoy creating jobs through expansion or creating better business efficiencies by leveraging supply chains, using advantages of scale, or protecting their position in the marketplace.

Growth might also be a do-or-die, an us-or-them, strategy. Growth in business is a way to ward off hostile competition, and may the youngest warrior win. Why the youngest? The older ones may be ready to sell or just unwilling to adapt to the changes happening around them. The younger ones are still hungry.

I find a healthier way to look at growth is to recognize that it doesn't always fit the dynamic stereotype of adding more personnel or establishing a larger share of the marketplace. In this regard, sometimes it helps to put on your x-ray goggles. You need to see avenues of growth not immediately obvious to everyone else.

Raises

Growth might simply mean giving everyone a raise. I'm unduly dedicated to the proposition that rewarding employees amply for their services is a critical business necessity. Your talent will flee the moment your competition catches up to you, so you better be ready to stay ahead of the curve on compensation rather than falling behind.

Benefits

Adding benefits to the compensation package is a form of growth that longtime employees appreciate. And, by the way, ask them what types of new benefits they'd appreciate before adding them.

They might ask for more time off. Sure, no employee who ever punched a clock would turn down more income, but this isn't always the best way to grow. Adding more paid time off (PTO) is a form of growth.

Training

This is a big one to me. Sending employees to take a seminar or course or paying for them to complete a degree is also a form of growth. Training in a variety of styles serves the employee directly, but it also serves the business.

Good References

Employers learn to accept the loss of staff. And there's always another employee willing to jump aboard a company that values their staff enough to help them grow as individuals. Giving your departing employees excellent references when they choose to move on is the right thing to do—if they weren't great, you would never have kept them on, right? Acknowledge that when they leave for greener pastures.

Community Involvement

I need to point out that benefiting the community around you is also a form of growth. You and your staff have a stake in the place—you probably live and work there, or at least your clients probably do. Ask your staff what type of involvement is dear to their hearts. Make your business a contributor to a better community.

Make Yourself Redundant

While you learn to cultivate your own interests, you need to know whether your business will survive without your presence on a day-to-day basis. We looked at the personal aspect of this issue when we discussed sabbaticals. Now it's about testing the efficiency of your business's process management. Will your systems perform when you walk away, or will you realize there are glaring holes in your processes?

Efficiencies are important when you answer the question of what your business is worth without you. A highly efficient business—one with systems—is far more valuable than one needing a captain at the helm every day. Test your systems by practicing walking away from the business. Yes, take that sabbatical. Practice taking time off. Take off an hour or two. Then go back to the office and survey the mayhem (or lack thereof). Did the place fall apart? What were the first few questions your staff asked you when you checked back in? Were they about a systems failure? Non-performing processes? Analyze it. Fix it. Then leave again.

One way or another, your staff will understand three things: You're not there sometimes, the show must go on anyway, and they have to (are allowed to) take ownership in your absence. Empower them. Provided you haven't got everyone over-working to begin with, this is a time to groom your replacement or replacements if the structure of the business pushes you in that direction.

Clearly, life is a trial by fire. It might feel like your business will burn down, blow up, or get beat up in your absence. Probably not. But the fail-safe formula for confronting this fear is to take small steps that challenge your assumptions, your staff, and your systems.

Chapter 11

Deciding When to Exit

Someday your turn will come. As an entrepreneur, you'll find yourself taking out that list of goals you wrote before you started this journey to see how you did. Did you accomplish your goals? Are some still half done or not done at all?

Many achievers know that little trick of patting yourself on the back. I've heard it said that crossing something off your to-do list is the payoff. It's the ritual that allows you to hum the *Rocky* theme music.

While we're at it, rituals are important. You can invent your own, and they don't have to be extravagant. That said, imagine someone patting you on the back. This might be the time to do that.

What will be the deciding factors in when you take your bow and exit stage left from your business? Let's look at some factors you might consider and sum things up.

Do You Still Love It?

There's no shame in admitting the thrill is gone. Many people eventually tire of the same ol', same ol'. The routine goes stale. Others burn out. Some jobs are intense, and you might reach a tipping point where the work that once rocked your boat now just feels like a chore. It doesn't do it for you anymore.

Some say there's no cure for this and it's simply time for a change. Whether you can pull that off or not is a big question (coming up), but burnout and interest fatigue are both very hard to reverse.

I suggest you reinvent the way you do your work and share your knowledge. One way of doing this is admittedly radical. You run the place, so you can, ostensibly, name your job. I'm not saying you can go back to parking cars, and I would be very reluctant to tell you to replace someone on your staff, but if the opportunity for a demotion comes up, that's something you can consider. These are other options that come to mind:

- Turn yourself into a fractional/part-time consultant to new entrepreneurs. You have direct, valuable knowledge to share with the world of business.

- Book yourself as a public speaker for conferences and symposiums.

- If you have a local college, a community college, or even an adult education night school in your area, find out whether they need a business teacher.

- Ask to join a for-profit or nonprofit board that would benefit from your insights and experience.

Any of these might allow you to hit that refresh button without exiting your business just yet.

How any of these changes could reflect on your own business is hard to say from a distance. You frequently test your process management, right? That means you already know whether you have a smoothly running operation that can survive your divided attention, with an administrator who keeps the machine humming.

Have You Saved Enough for Retirement?

This is the million-dollar question when exiting your business: Have you accumulated enough wealth to retire?

This is what Dad (the attorney I told you about) was asking Son who wanted to retire in his late twenties. It's a valid question at any age. Americans are not good savers if you believe the statistics out there.

American business owners generally struggle to save adequately for retirement compared to employees with company-sponsored retirement plans. A survey I read showed that 30 percent of small business owners aren't confident they're saving enough for retirement.[16]

As a business owner, I see the temptations: We prefer reinvesting profits in the business over socking them away in a retirement savings account. And while a lot of homeowners say, "My home is my retirement plan; I'm going to sell it and downsize," business owners say the sale of their business is their whole retirement plan (and because of that, they fail to diversify their investments). But the research shows that as many

---

16   Steve Strauss, "How Do You Save for Retirement When You Are Self-Employed? Use the 10% Rule," *USA Today*, July 24, 2019, https://www.usatoday.com/story/money/usaandmain/2019/07/10/small-business-owner-retirement/1688316001.

as 80 percent of business owners never sell because their personal wealth is tied to the company.

Look at March 2020 and that whole year-plus of quarantine and pandemic. You couldn't have *given* your business away then. How do you know you'll be able to sell the business profitably when you happen to be ready?[17]

Avoid guessing about your financial readiness. Hopefully by now this is a question you bring to your trusty financial advisor, whom I hope you've been working with for at least a decade.

Are You Satisfied?

Study your list of goals again in all their six or more dimensions, and look for the non-monetary factors. In other words, instead of only assessing your finances, ask yourself, *Am I satisfied?*

Satisfaction is a big deal: Did you learn to play that musical instrument, write that novel, run in that marathon, and go to *every* one of your kids' ball games and theater productions as you intended? In other words, have you enjoyed the journey or just focused on work,

---

17 Justin Goodbread, "Warning: Your Business Is Not a Retirement Fund!," *Kiplinger*, December 11, 2021, https://www.kiplinger. com/business/small-business/entrepreneurship/603901/ warning-your-business-is-not-a-retirement-fund.

work, work? Have you truly stopped to smell the roses, to admire the life you have built—and enjoyed the journey you've been on?

That isn't such a crazy thing to ask. Haven't I been asking it in all these pages?

Could You Be an Employee Again?

We get used to the perks of being king or queen of the realm, don't we? We get a lot of attention, farm out the parts of our jobs we don't like, have our names on signs in the parking lot. We buy nice desks and chairs for ourselves and enjoy big windows in our C-suite offices. Others are accountable to us, not the reverse.

Ah, the high life!

On the other hand, if the right juicy offer comes up, or if that burnout catches you at a younger age than you planned in your exit goal—could you consider taking orders instead of giving them? Could you be on someone else's payroll?

You need to think hard about this one. Do some reality checks. Go back to all those goals you wrote. Look at the ones still unachieved. But also look at how far you've come.

The news flash, which you probably already know, is that humans are not designed to just sit on a beach and listen to the waves month after month. We usually can't afford that anyway, but the truth is humans need something to do. The two things that keep us going, according to Sigmund Freud (or some such guru I recently read about), are love and work. Look around; we're a fairly industrious species. If we can't find a job, we plant gardens. We don't like to sit still.

Furthermore, for most of us, work is our biggest source of excitement. Real work. Money changing hands. Work that means getting dirty and seeing the fruits of our labor. That's right, it gets lonely out there. And boring. And isolating. And it makes your back hurt. Before you leap into your post-business life, check your side mirrors. You never know. When all is said and done, it might just be time to work for someone else. It might feel strange to wear those shoes again. Think long and hard about it.

But, again, the formula presents itself. If you're looking for something to do in retirement, you started looking too late. May I remind you of the multidimensional goals I suggested to you? I dread the idea of going home after my retirement party, sitting on the bed, and realizing I have no plans for tomorrow. I imagine you do too.

We know the Bockstahler formula by now:

- Multidimensional goals that allow you to enjoy the journeys of life *and* business in a side-by-side synergy of balance
- Process management for your business so you can step away at need or at will
- Goals regularly reviewed to make sure you stay the course or change direction as the need arises
- Incremental process management improvements
- Bite-sized risk-taking until you know where you are

You also need to start early. All along, even before you open your business, you should be doing the following:

- Cultivating hobbies and leisure activities
- Cultivating health practices and self-awareness
- Planning ahead by delegating to experts and staff, strategizing, and continuously reviewing plans

Reacting without planning is relying on luck and is usually an outcome of defeatism. Like business, many hobbies are not as easy as they look. You might want to get all that fumbling around out of the way so you don't find yourself thinking *Geez, this is harder than I thought* in your first week of retirement.

A good hobby for you, of course, is the one in which you actually enjoy the learning curve. The modern age would have no pianos or violins if learning wasn't fun. Nevertheless, if you're not hobby-prone or exercise-prone, the time to try all those things is when you're young so you don't hit the snooze button fifteen times before leaping (or maybe falling) out of bed the first day after you retire. That's all I'm saying.

And, as you get up, pat yourself on the back. You've earned it. Then get out there and play the game.

Conclusion

I want to talk again a little about when Frank and I started Amata. My goals for my life were clear to me: I knew that I wanted to have children and raise them by my wife's side. I wanted to go to every Cubs home game. Then I started thinking about how any business of mine had to serve those goals and others I had identified in the six dimensions I mentioned to you and give me the time freedom to achieve them. Those things were reflections of my desire for life balance, so they were, in a very real sense, my end goal.

Happily, Frank and I agreed we both wanted to have our time freedom. We would *not* be the ones serving the business.

I think you see that my core reasons for starting a business did not include this big vision of making millions and millions of dollars. I had a vision of enjoying my whole multidimensional life. I would be supporting my wonderful family through a successful and profitable business and having the free time I wanted with those I love. The money came. Yes, it did. But I got my priorities straight first, then built a business that would serve them.

Looking back and looking at my life today, I don't think I could work for someone else again. It's so liberating to set my own schedule. Granted, there are difficulties to it from time to time just like in anything else, but I take them in stride. The payoff is worth it.

Whatever your reason for starting your business, I firmly believe the business will serve you when you write that reason down as a goal. We forget what we don't write and reread, and it will be your GPS directions to business operations (process management) that don't need you in the office all the time.

I say this from experience: If I hadn't looked at my two dozen multidimensional goals frequently and regularly, I would have forgotten what they were from week to week and month to month. I would have veered off course. If that had happened, my family would have forgotten what I looked and sounded like. The Cubs would have had to get along without my cheers. When I'm six or eight months into a year, I don't want to risk forgetting what my goal for the year is, so I reread it over and over. It's my GPS—another tool that serves me and not the other way around.

When you're trying to figure out what you want in life, you should focus on your endgame first and foremost. If you're thinking about starting a business, do it for the right reasons. I hope I've given you some insight in these pages as to how to achieve that.

I seriously think I've made every mistake known to man. But I've learned some valuable things from those mistakes. I hope I've shown you how to make a living, build a business that serves your life goals, and have a great life that's balanced in all the ways that matter to you.

About the Author

Ron Bockstahler is a father to six children and husband to a loving wife. He's an athlete and entrepreneur. With a unique perspective on life, he started his business, Amata Holdings LLC, more than twenty-two years ago with the twin goals of raising a family and attending as many home Chicago Cubs games as possible.

Throughout his career, Ron has maintained a relentless focus on setting and achieving life goals. After dropping out of high school to support his young family, he returned to finish his diploma, graduating with his class. To pay for college and gain the discipline to thrive there, Ron joined the US Marine Corps, where he served four years as an enlisted marine. After his tour, he attended Northern Illinois University, where he completed his degree in less than three years.

After graduating from college, he took a position as a copier salesperson, where he cut his teeth and learned what it took to succeed in business. Within a corporate career spanning fourteen years with two companies, Ron worked his way up from copier salesman to the C-suite, always setting written goals and working tirelessly to achieve them.

After he spent most of his career as a self-proclaimed workaholic, running his own business taught Ron to appreciate the value of a balanced life. For more than twenty-two years, he has worked to balance running a successful company, raising six children, maintaining a healthy marriage, and working to become a competitive athlete. During these years, he has competed in seven full Ironman races and numerous triathlons and marathons—with more to come.

He likes to say, "Life is about the journey. Enjoy it, and don't be in a hurry for it to end!"